Jean Paul Gaultier

Jean Paul Gaultier

Colin McDowell

CASSELL&CO

Contents

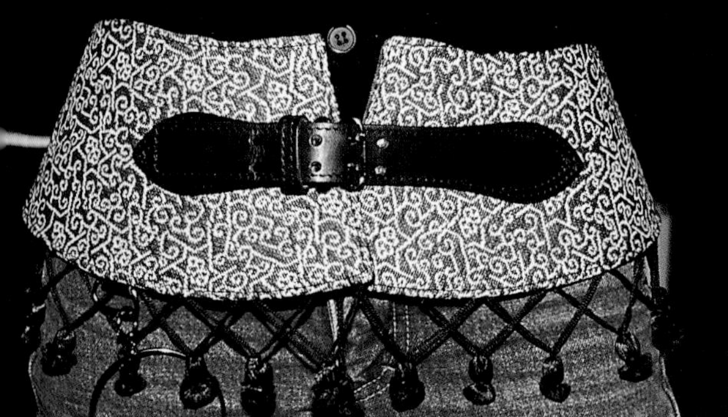

'As a ch
a
surroun
by ad

1

THE LITTLE KING

THROW A STICK IN THE FASHION WORLD and all will give chase, barking nervously, afraid that a fresh movement might find them lagging behind; alarmed in case a new terminology should convey nothing to them. Fashion thrives on insecurity. It thrives on instant decisions memorably conveyed. It thrives on assumptions, judgements and attributions more acceptable the slicker they are. Its pronouncements present an insider's code, a shorthand which frequently develops into a permanent *aide memoire* for those who lack the energy and perception to reappraise, reassess and rename.

No one knows who first used the shorthand epithet *enfant terrible* to address – or even fail to address – the oblique genius of Jean Paul Gaultier. It happened at the end of the seventies or beginning of the eighties, a time when Gaultier's fashion creations, revolutionary and even anti-social in viewpoint, to many verging on the prurient and scatalogical in obsessions, were sufficiently different from the rest of the high fashion output of Paris for *enfant terrible* to serve a purpose and convey a meaning to the undemanding. It was also a time when Jean Paul was still young enough for the expression to have a basis in fact.

That was over twenty years ago, but Jean Paul Gaultier is still described by far too many journalists, far too many times, as *enfant terrible*, although, as he is now almost fifty, it has become a grotesquely inappropriate sobriquet – except that, continuing as he first set out, he still dances to the beat of his own drum, using steps conceived by him alone, to be defiantly and dazzlingly performed across the trivial, repetitive and recycled face of international fashion. Jean Paul Gaultier is even less of a conformist today than he was in his *enfant terrible* days. Age has done nothing to wither, nor custom to stale, his infinite variety.

Jean Paul Gaultier today has the confidence of the successful man, although he claims to be shy and insecure. Certainly, he was both when he was young. By his own admission, he lacked even a child's social aplomb and was happiest in his own world of make-believe and dreams of impossible futures. Uncertain of the reception of some of the thoughts which moved him most deeply as a boy, he kept them to himself, hidden from the world, part of a very important internal dialogue for no one's ears but his. An outsider, he whispered solely to himself of his secret

'School was a lonely place'

ALTHOUGH his schooldays were not the happiest of his life, Jean Paul Gaultier has frequently used the memories of school uniforms and how they looked after vigorous play or unauthorized fights in order to create an unbuttoned, *dégagé* appearance with a certain sexual frisson, as he did for his Spring-Summer 1993 collection. (*Photo: Niall McInerney*)

world. Physically, he was convinced that he was too ugly and ordinary to inspire friendship, let alone love, and he tried to blend, to hide and disappear. But although Jean Paul Gaultier's childhood was secret, it was not lonely. In place of the schoolfriends he rarely made, he had his parents and, above all, his grandmother, who remained a lasting and powerful influence on him.

Jean Paul Gaultier, an only child, was born in Paris in 1952. In Paris, and yet *not* in Paris. If that city conjures up fifties visions of the elegance of Place Vendôme, the spaciousness of the Champs Elysées and the nostalgia of the Palais Royale, it was not the Paris of Gaultier and his family. Their Paris was the southern suburbs of the city, beyond what is now the *Peripherique*, the outer ring-road at that time undreamed of, let alone built, in an area called Arcueil. On his streets little Jean Paul saw no chic women dressed in the post-New Look fashions of the grand couturiers, carrying tiny but perfectly wrapped parcels from their perfumiers. To most of the citizens of Arcueil, the Paris of elegance and perfection was as remote as Indo-China. It wasn't the sort of suburb like, for example, Pinner, North London, from which, in the fifties, people daily travelled to work in the West End of London and returned trailing at least some of the clouds of glory from the sophisticated centre.

Most of the people of Arcueil stayed put, working locally; in the majority of cases, within walking distance or a short tram-ride of work. It was a predominantly working-class area, with its small middle-class element playing minor roles at the bottom end of the professional scale. The bank manager would not be likely to live in Arcueil, although the clerk might and the guard or porter would. Self-contained and self-possessed, its people didn't look upwards and outwards, as they certainly would in Pinner. They had their own energy, separate and independent of that in the streets of the centre of the city, and took pride in the fact that virtually everything they could possibly require could be obtained in their neighbourhood – including work.

Looking back, Jean Paul feels that Arcueil, gritty and grey with the smoke from the factory chimneys, would have made a marvellous setting for a *Nouvelle Vague* film of the time, concerned with the realities of working-class life. But he could see, even as a child, that it had a certain

'My parents were terrified at

heavy nineteenth-century nobility with its viaduct and church. In fact, the man who has claimed 'I'm completely urban' knows that much of his character and many of his attitudes were formed by Arcueil, the basis for his idealization of the suburbs after he had grown up and moved away from them. Certainly, Arcueil formed a comfortably reliable background for a childhood which might seem lonely but was certainly not reclusive. In fact, although he did not find it easy to make friends at school, he was rarely alone, living as he did in an almost exclusively adult world, as only children often do. As he says, 'As a child, I was a little king, surrounded more by adults than children.'

Jean Paul's father, Paul, was a book-keeper – a respectable job for a first-generation educated man from a working-class background. Jean Paul recalls him as being 'very sweet and kind', although he has also hinted at tensions by referring in interviews to a gambling problem which kept the family poor. His mother, Solange, worked as a secretary and Jean Paul found her family background much more interesting than his father's. His maternal grandfather's father, who married an English-woman, had a cork factory in the Lot-et-Garonne. Jean Paul's grandfather was a traveller who set off for America in the early 1900s and then spent twelve years in London. He was away from France for eighteen years, and tales of his exploits fascinated the young Jean Paul. In 1958, when Jean Paul was only six, the old man went to Brussels for the Universal Exhibition, entirely by himself, despite the fact that he was over eighty. Although a quaintly old-fashioned figure in Jean Paul's eyes, he had a subliminal influence, because Jean Paul Gaultier has been an inveterate traveller for all of his adult life and, although he laughed at his grandfather when he tried to teach him English, Jean Paul speaks it fluently but with an accent which suggests he learned by listening to Maurice Chevalier singing with a marble in his mouth.

Jean Paul's parents lived a private and enclosed life, discouraging casual visits, although they were aware of the world opening up in the mid-1960s when Jean Paul was on the brink of his teenage years. The growth in package holidays and cheap flights made holidays to new destinations accessible to all classes. For the first time ever, it was possible for ordinary French families to forsee the possibility of holidays abroad,

my becoming a fashion designer'

GAULTIER's greatest comfort as a child was talking to his teddy bear. This picture, taken in 1984, referred to those past days but gave no hint of the transformation in his appearance which was soon to come when he went blonde and began to create his 'signature' look of matelot jersey and Doc Marten's. (*Photo: Patrick Jackson*)

and the family talked a lot about 'dream' destinations, especially Spain. In fact, Jean Paul's father hoped that his son might some day study to be a Spanish teacher. It was not something which appealed to Jean Paul, who has said, 'I first wanted to be a cook and make patisseries' – as an adult, Gaultier is addicted to cakes – 'then a hairdresser and, after that, I began to want to make clothes'.

In order to understand how that idea was subconsciously nurtured, it is necessary to turn to the single most important influence not only on Gaultier's childhood but on his own whole life: Marie Garrabe, his maternal grandmother, with whom the family spent most weekends. Gaultier has admitted in many interviews that, for him, school was a lonely place. Different, hopeless at sport, he now says that, 'as a child I was very boring'. But he had a champion, a guide and a comforter in his grandmother. He adored her and loved to stay with her in her comfortable little house, enjoying the central heating, a great luxury in the 1950s, hardly known in any homes other than those of the comfortable middle class. She also had a television and a fridge – again, rarities for the average French family in that period.

Marie Garrabe was a local 'character'. A bit of a mystic, a hypnotist and an early practitioner of alternative healing, she also gave beauty advice and practical help with things like home perms, as well as telling fortunes and reading Tarot cards. Jean Paul spent every Thursday at her house, arriving on Wednesday and frequently feigning sickness on Friday so that he didn't have to go to school and could stretch the visit into the weekend. He loved the atmosphere in the rather heavy, dark rooms, and the little bourgeois decorative touches such as the lace tablecloths, the old-fashioned lamps and heavy bedspreads; but, above all, he loved to watch his grandmother as she ministered to her 'clients'. As he explained to *Women's Wear Daily*, 'From her I learned the importance of physical appearance as it relates to the interior life – the importance of attitudes, gestures, movement and how everything is connected.'

What she was running was, in essence, a home beauty parlour – one of the exciting postwar discoveries for ordinary women in Britain and Europe, although a standard part of prewar life in America. Jean Paul loved the smells of the preparations she used, even the bitter smell of the

The day that Jean Paul first saw the Folies-Bergère (*left*) on television changed his life. Fascinated by the beauty and colour of the costumes – not to mention their sexuality – he couldn't stop drawing them, even though it got him into serious trouble at school. The elements of fantasy – feathers, cockades and exotic head-dresses – have been used so frequently by the couturier that they are now recognized almost as staples of his collections.

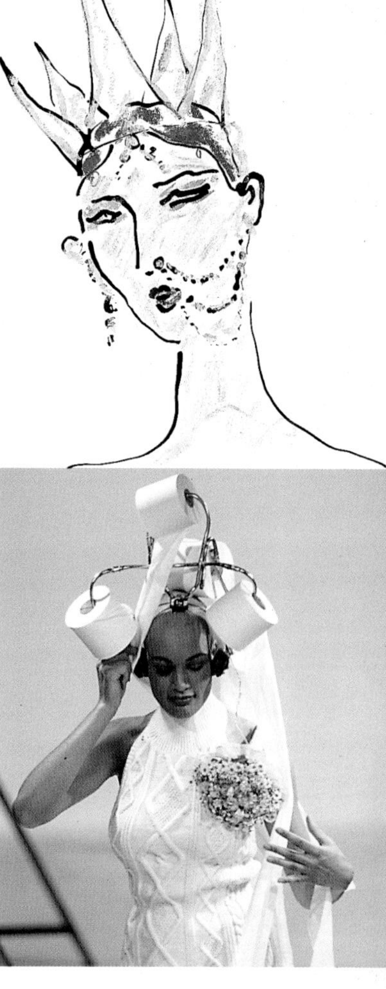

The Spring-Summer collection of 1994 (*illustration top right*) included 'Tattooings', which according to the press release, was about 'romanticism and spirituality or Joan of Arc via Benares or Gulliver via Lilliput'. The Autumn-Winter 1992–3 collection, which contained this head-dress and Aran knit ensemble (*right*), was dedicated to the Europe of the future, mixing races and the influence of immigrants with the popular traditions and folklores of each country.
(*Photo: Niall McInerney; drawing: Gladys Perint Palmer*)

home perm solutions which gave off an odour part ammonia and part sulphur. But mostly he loved sitting quietly drawing and becoming of no more significance to the women than the furniture. 'I would draw them how, according to my imagination, I wanted them to look – in evening gowns, perhaps with incredible hairstyles,' he recalls. Gossip about loves, local scandals, talk of illness and death: all the news of the town was aired as his grandmother advised and performed. More importantly, as he sat ostensibly watching television but with one ear cocked to the talk, he learned of female problems and became aware of the great feminine mysteries. In many ways the classic education of a childhood invert, it was also the grounding for the future designer's particular approach to femininity, although it was no help to him at school. 'I was very *au courant* in the problems of the heart,' he says, 'but the problems of football didn't interest me at all.'

As he was drawing, Jean Paul was creating his own surrogate world, as vibrant and real for him as the secret world of the Brontës who, as children wrote romantic tales for each other, in miniature. Gaultier's world was quite as private but it was very much based on the here and now. Like many only children who find it difficult to make contacts with their peers, he had a vivid life of the imagination and, inevitably, a 'best friend'. His teddy bear, Nana, was his constant companion as he lounged, drawing, on a sofa. He talked to him in whispers as the women were drinking coffee and anxiously waiting for the outcome of the cards – or the perm, as his grandmother took out the rollers and pins. And if Jean Paul saw Marilyn Monroe on the television, Nana became her in his imagination. When he watched his grandmother giving a colouring treatment to a neighbour's hair, Nana must have one too. And so it went on, with the boy retreating further into a fantasy world.

Why did his grandmother indulge him so much? Gaultier believes that it is because, having lost her first daughter, who died in 1914, she had a mystical belief that her grandson was, if not a reincarnation, then some sort of cipher, leading her to the past. She allowed him to get away with everything, even agreeing to his cutting and colouring her hair, and helping her with the clients. Above all, she allowed him to watch anything he wished on television, at any hour, even though cinema cards had been introduced in 1950 in France to protect children from screen violence and what at the time was considered explicit sex.

Apart from television, what were the cultural influences on Jean Paul Gaultier, embryonic couturier, in his late childhood and early teens? The answer is that they were two-fold. His grandmother was his link to the popular entertainment of the past. She would fiddle with the radio until she found Charles Trenet singing his great hit *La Mer*. Or it could be

Maurice Chevalier, Jean Sablon, or the incomparable Piaf. It might be a newer but very traditional French music hall entertainer such as Yves Montand or Piaf's ex-pianist Charles Aznavour, or even Les Companions de la Chansons. But Jean Paul also did his fiddling until he found the performers *he* liked, pre-eminently Francoise Hardy, whose clothes excited him as much as her voice, Juliette Greco and a rather vulgar but very entertaining singer called Shiela. He had his own little record-player and one of his favourite discs was *Eloise* – he still knows the words by heart.

Jean Paul Gaultier remembers a seminal moment in his cultural and sentimental education: the time when he went with his grandmother to visit one of her younger clients. Her radio was tuned to a very different channel and, for the first time, he heard the Rolling Stones singing *Satisfaction*. It was a revelation. 'I didn't understand a word,' he confesses. 'But I understood the strength even though I'd never heard anything like it before. For me, I now realize, its impact was sexual. It was very exciting. I felt that something was going on inside me, something beyond my control. There were things in that song that I wanted to know about, must know about.'

And television continued to feed his fantasies. Left to his own devices, he watched programmes forbidden to children, those bearing the infamous white square for parental guidance. That is how he came to see a documentary about the Folies-Bergère. He adored the glitter and gold, but he especially fell in love with the feathers. It was the beginning of what he now sees as his sexual education, linked with 'gay fantasies of men who show a certain femininity in their clothes, although I always wanted to balance it with a strong masculinity. I have never wanted to show drag queens or transvestites in my collections. I'm not interested in men trying to look like women'.

Such considerations were in the future. His clandestine introduction to the Folies-Bergère produced different, more immediate results. In school the day after the broadcast he was sketching figures inspired by the costumes he'd seen. Suddenly, an outraged teacher pounced. To teach him a lesson, she pinned the offending drawing on his back and made him parade through all of the classrooms so that his fellow pupils could laugh at him. But what could have been a deeply searing, humiliating

IT IS EASY to imagine that Gaultier is only interested in the glitter of paillettes and bugle beads but that shows only one of his many creative strands. He is equally at home with natural materials such as raffia and straw, even when they turn out to be simulations in rubber and plastic. All pictures are from the Spring-Summer 1992 collection which paid tribute to extravagance and the elegance of Modernism (*Photos: Niall McInerney; drawing: Gladys Perint Palmer*)

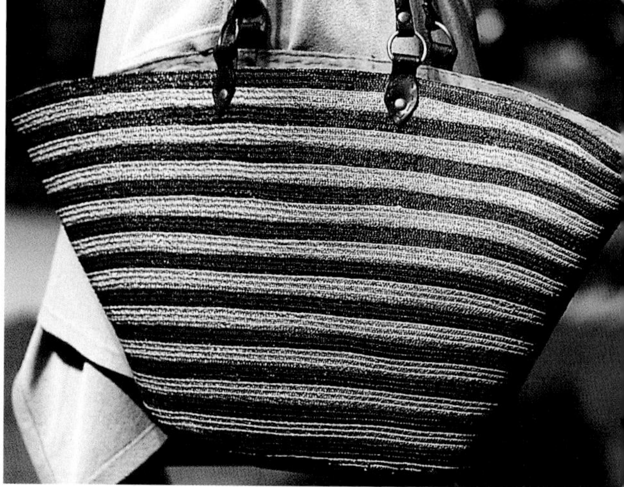

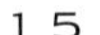

experience for the boy in fact turned into something very positive. Jean Paul Gaultier now looks at the failure of his early school years with a certain laconic irony. 'I was not popular,' he admits. 'I was no Cantona.' But on that fateful morning, he became something else: a local hero. 'Of course,' he concedes, 'the children laughed. But not at me – with me. I could sense it. So humiliation turned to triumph and I was proud to let everyone see my drawing. I had become a sort of personality.' More than that, the television programme and the subsequent fiasco so hardened his determination that he was no longer afraid to admit his passion for clothes and spectacle. No more secret little drawings. From now on, he showed his grandmother and his parents almost everything he drew. And, even though, in his words, his mother and father were 'terrified at my becoming a fashion designer', the die was cast.

He had his first trip to the music hall at Chatelet and cried emotionally at the excitement and beauty of it all. The star was Andre Dassary and Gaultier remembers how, almost in a trance, he watched as actors flew across the stage, attached by invisible strings. The Moulin Rouge; the Folies; the Lido: he loved them all, totally unconcerned at how politically incorrect their projection of women was, especially in the light of Simone de Beauvoir's seminal feminist text, *The Second Sex*, which has exerted

an enormous influence since its publication in 1948.

'I trained in couture,' Gaultier says today. 'It is my base. When I first started to really become interested in fashion, I couldn't believe there was anything else – or ever could be. In the sixties there were strong ready-to-wear designers like Emmanuelle Khanh, who had been a model at Balenciaga, and Sonia Rykiel in Paris, with Mary Quant in London, but for most of the decade, fashion, as far as French TV or magazines were concerned, was haute couture.' Bored with school and totally obsessed with fashion, he pretended to be sick so that he could stay at home and draw. Is memory deceiving him when he says that, in order to buy time, he consulted his grandmother's medical books and became sufficiently *au fait* with the symptoms of rheumatic fever to fool the doctors for three years? Did he really, as he later told *Gay Times*, steal fashion magazines to

GAULTIER HAS always decried the simplistic approach to the sexes which dresses women as sex objects but doesn't bring the same attitude to male dress. He highlights the male bulge as an erotic zone in exactly the same way in which other designers pinpoint areas of the female anatomy. These looks add long slinky gloves for elegance, half hide the face for allure, use fringing for titilation and add gold for glamour. All are acceptable – even clichéd – elements of female dress but cause unease when worn by men. That is because male dress has no vocabulary of seduction, a fact Jean Paul deplores.

ALL OF THE ABOVE are from Gaultier's menswear collection Spring-Summer 1989, called 'Baroque Western', which looked at 'the mysteries of the West... and the urban cowboy'. (*Photos: Niall McInerney*)

'I love to put some cute guys in my shows'

'I like strong women'

feed and educate his passion, because he didn't have the money to buy them? Either claim might well be true or not, but their importance lies with the fact that they show the dedication and determination of the teenager who had found the thing which moved and inspired him. Fashion had become the grand obsession.

But it was a particular and specific form of fashion. Throughout the sixties, Jean Paul Gaultier's interest was in couture – the exclusive, high fashion end of the business where clothes are made for individual clients, using the very best of materials, involving several fittings and with most of the sewing done by hand. An expensive, time-consuming privilege of the rich, costing a great deal of money, it was, even in the sixties, a dying art form. Life's pace and rising costs made it insupportable for even the wealthy but, for a long time, it was to the young Gaultier everything fashion should be – exemplified in *Falbalas*, a film made in 1944 about the life of a fictional couturier, starring Micheline Presle and Raymond Rouleau, with costumes by Rochas. It is a film he has seen many times. As a teenager, he found it literally entrancing. Here was his dream world made flesh on the screen. Everything he felt he needed to know about the inner workings of a couture house and the creation of a collection seemed to be there, including the intrigues and tensions which were made much of by a script which, to modern eyes, seems ludicrous.

But not to the teenage Gaultier, who swallowed the drama as uncritically as he adored the dresses. He has said that, for a suburban boy from an unsophisticated background, *Falbalas* was literally a how-to-do-it primer. From it, he learned how a grand couturier walked, talked and created. He discovered the elegance of the impossibly perfect model and, above all, he saw how clothes behaved in movement – especially clothes made of delicate and expensive fabrics – something he could not learn from the static pictures he saw in newspapers and magazines.

If *Falbalas* was an inspiration to him, it was the other sources which provided the practical knowledge he craved. It is not easy for us today to imagine how constrained and limited a young man like Gaultier was in the sixties. With no money and little confidence, he didn't frequent the milieu of the fashionable, so how was he to learn what fashion was? He did so through newspapers, but it is a measure of his lack of sophistication

THE PREDATORY woman is a fantasy which modern designers frequently find exciting. Jean Paul Gaultier adds pieces of armour to corsetted and diaphanous femininity in order to increase the strength of his message. This powerful homage to Joan of Arc is a corset dress accessorised with armour, and was created for 'Tattooings'. Gaultier's Spring-Summer 1994 collection.
(*Photo: Niall McInerney*)

'I simply have fun with

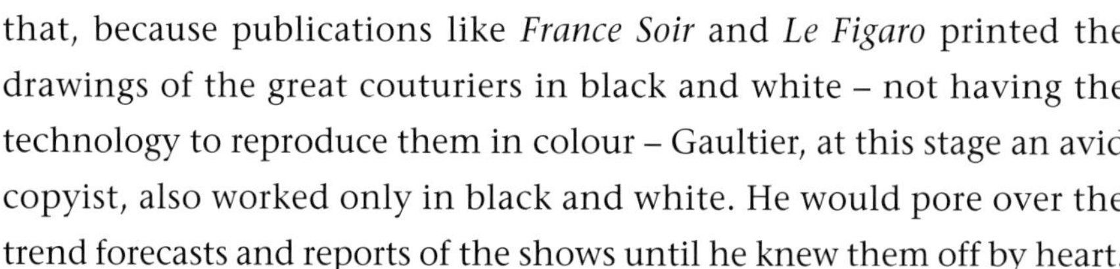

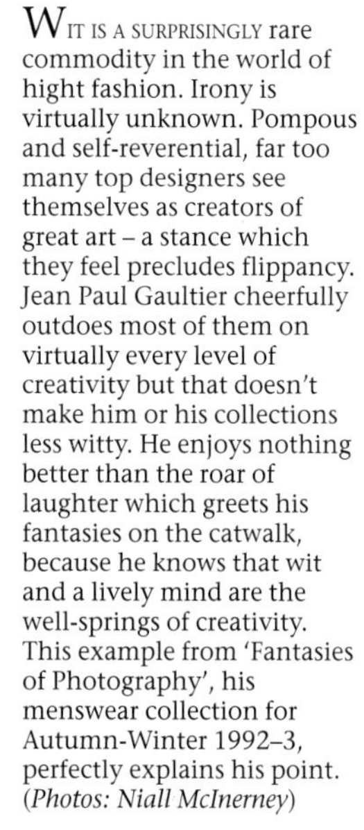

Wit is a surprisingly rare commodity in the world of hight fashion. Irony is virtually unknown. Pompous and self-reverential, far too many top designers see themselves as creators of great art – a stance which they feel precludes flippancy. Jean Paul Gaultier cheerfully outdoes most of them on virtually every level of creativity but that doesn't make him or his collections less witty. He enjoys nothing better than the roar of laughter which greets his fantasies on the catwalk, because he knows that wit and a lively mind are the well-springs of creativity. This example from 'Fantasies of Photography', his menswear collection for Autumn-Winter 1992–3, perfectly explains his point. *(Photos: Niall McInerney)*

that, because publications like *France Soir* and *Le Figaro* printed the drawings of the great couturiers in black and white – not having the technology to reproduce them in colour – Gaultier, at this stage an avid copyist, also worked only in black and white. He would pore over the trend forecasts and reports of the shows until he knew them off by heart.

And then he put his knowledge to practical use. He began to design whole collections in page after page of drawings detailing everything he imagined would appear on a runway, including accessories and jewellery. He worked exactly as he assumed a couturier did when creating a collection, producing as many as 300 drawings which he would then edit down to the eighty or so that would be his 'show'. It was all supposition and imagination, of course – the only show was the one which took place in his head, although he did obtain some feedback and encouragement from a friend of his mother who worked for a small periodical called *L'Echo de la Mode*. She was sufficiently impressed with his ideas to ask him to put on paper some suggestions for children's clothing.

Gradually, his parameters were extended. He began to look at *Elle* and *Marie-Claire*, both magazines at the cutting edge of the new prêt-à-porter but were conscious of the importance of couture for things other than clothing, such as make-up and beauty products, strong sources of advertising revenue. Editorially, they were forward-looking and could see the new informality which was developing as vibrant, young fashion houses and ready-to-wear firms began to spring up – Dorothée Bis, Christiane Bailly, Cacharel and Daniel Hechter. Gaultier was aware of them but, as he has said, for him, 'Couture was still fashion. I couldn't imagine that anything would ever take its place.' If this shows a blindness to what now seem self-evident facts, he wasn't so entirely in love with the grand fashion houses not to have opinions.

'It was Yves Saint Laurent and Christian Dior who made me dream,' he recalls. 'I really wanted to do things like they did. What Chanel did, I always found "old" and, although I now find Balenciaga fascinating, in the sixties, to be honest, he seemed to me to be doing things which didn't connect with my ideas of fashion, any more than Givenchy, whose clothes were very "old lady" to me.' He could make such judgements because his fashion sense was becoming more sophisticated, honed by an clothes'

For Spring-Summer 1992, Gaultier took as his inspiration for his menswear collection 'the city gym teacher mixed with Casanova' and called it 'Casanova at the Gymnasium'. It was full of Tom of Finland fantasies of the male as hunk. (*Photo: Niall McInerney; drawing: Tom of Finland*)

increasing number of influences. His grandmother now had a cleaning woman, Yvonne, who had been a *premier d'atelier* at the old-fashioned but respected fashion house of Paquin, founded in 1891 by Madame Paquin. A true ally, Yvonne took his drawings seriously and helped with practical suggestions. But what Jean Paul found most thrilling were her anecdotes of the life of a great fashion house, dramas and disasters included.

French television featured Paris fashion week in the sixties, as it does now. Jean Paul watched the programmes avidly. Couture presentations in those days were calm, even austere occasions, with little of the hysteria and contrived atmosphere of today's shows. Middle-aged ladies, sensibly dressed, sat on discreet gold chairs while each model, with a number and usually a name, was presented individually – and normally in silence. The fashion show had its own rhythm, beginning with clothes suitable for smart morning and luncheon wear, followed by afternoon and cocktail dresses and rounded off by evening wear – important, extravagant and theatrical. Gaultier's imaginary dream fashion shows were presented at exactly the same rhythm. He went further, and even worked out which outfit would be best for each newspaper or magazine.

His discovery of *L'Officiel de la Couture et de la Mode de Paris* in 1968 was a watershed moment. Dedicated, as its title makes clear, to promoting French fashion around the world, *L'Officiel* was the bible of the trade. Its glamorous matte black-and-white photographs and its eloquently informative fashion illustrations were used as aide memoire, taste-maker and inspiration by tailors, little dressmakers and the dress trade at all levels and in all countries which possessed a fashion industry. In addition to its editorial pages – which spoke with total authority – its advertising was largely trade-oriented, with a heavy emphasis on furriers and fabric manufacturers. From them, Jean Paul learned not only the names but also the specialities of the great fabric houses which, for couture, were almost as important as the names of the grand couturiers – Ducharne, Bianchini Ferier and Staron for Lyon silks and Rodier, Lesur and Leonard et Cie for fine wools.

Gaultier really felt that he was becoming part of the couture world he had dreamed of for so long. As he has admitted, 'I still hardly knew the names in prêt-à-porter but I knew all the gossip in haute couture – or

OFTEN CRITICIZED for making fun of sexuality, of confusing gender definitions and making men and women – but most often men – look ridiculous, Gaultier is happy to give himself the same treatment. He loves dressing up, whether as the Princess of Wales or as a cleaning woman. For the MTV fashion and music awards in 1995, he wore a variety of costumes to show that dressing up or stripping down can be fun. (*Photos: Big Pictures*)

'People are too ready to classify as vulgar something that is strange and incomprehensible'

thought I did – by reading snippets about the goings-on at Patou, Ricci or whoever.' In fact, he soaked up whatever the magazines wrote, never questioning or criticizing what they said or chose to feature. When *Jardin des Modes*, for example, marked a dress 'Our Choice', he automatically assumed that it was the best from the whole collection, being totally unaware of the commercial pressures which might have influenced such an editorial decision. It didn't matter that he was so naive. His eye was being trained by knowledgeable and experienced journalists – although it was a very selective eye. Gaultier would hardly bother to look at the prêt-à-porter pictures, usually found at the end of the editorial pages. His passion was satisfied by the prestigious first pages, normally devoted to the grandeur of haute couture.

But magazines were expensive and pocket money tight, so buying the collections issue of *L'Officiel* – fat, juicy and expensive – or *Jardin des Modes* never became a routine. The issue was always a privilege, excitement and joy to be read a thousand times. As was Francois Boucher's

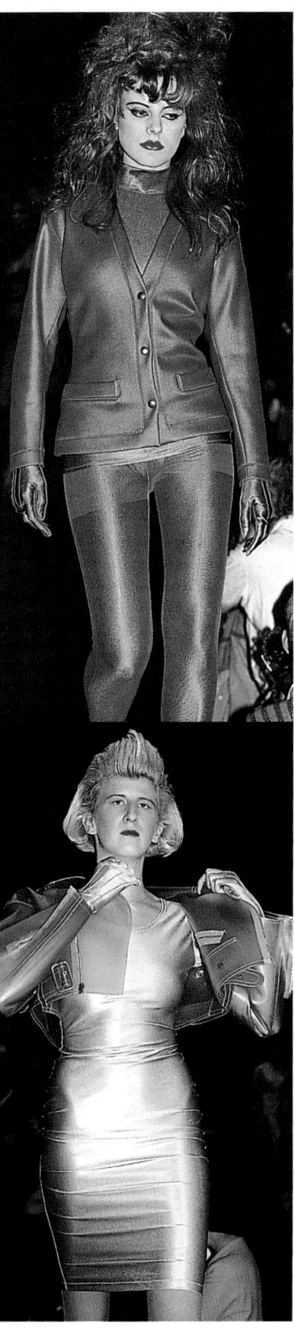

monumental *History of Costume in the West*, which was published in 1966. It also became compulsive reading for Gaultier.

Things were going well for him. Although the family took holidays in Spain and Jean Paul accompanied his grandmother to the mud baths in the Pays Basque, talk of his becoming a Spanish teacher faded before the overwhelming evidence of his enthusiasm for fashion – and his increasingly obvious design talent. It was a big breakthrough when he began to design dresses for his mother, which were made up by a friend of hers. He admits now that most of the skill was hers and the final product bore – perhaps mercifully – little relation to his original drawing. 'But', as he says, 'honour was satisfied. I had my first client. So it didn't matter, really.'

But it did. His mother's willingness to indulge her son was a huge psychological fillip for his aspirations. To his delight, the next stage was strong parental encouragement for the idea that he should try to sell some sketches in order to supplement his pocket money. Jean Paul leapt at the idea enthusiastically, even though his first attempt, encouraged by an acquaintance of his mother's who was a *modeliste* at Dior, had a disappointing result. She had taken some of his drawings to show to Marc Bohan, design director at Dior, appointed after the house had sacked Yves Saint Laurent. Austere and classic, it was inevitable that he would find Gaultier's exuberant and arresting ideas – which Jean Paul thought dramatic – merely vulgar. The intermediary returned with the edict: Gaultier's designs were not in the spirit of Monsieur Bohan's design approach for Dior and, in any case, his design *atelier* was at full strength and required no additional team members. But she returned with something else, which was her steadfast conviction that a young man as talented as Jean Paul Gaultier should not be discouraged so easily. She urged him to send his drawings to other fashion houses but cautioned that they must fit in with the spirit of the house.

It was a lesson well learned and Gaultier rationalized his drawings, making piles which he felt would be suitable for different houses, such as Louis Feraud, Courrèges and Cardin. Terrified of rejection, he didn't dare to deliver them in person. He sent them off in batches by post to twenty-seven fashion houses and waited to see if there would be any response.

WITH THE development of new fabrics and materials in the past twenty years, surfaces have become an area of fashion excitement. Often derivatives of plastic or rubber, they bring new areas of sexuality to the fore. Things which even recently would have embarrassed by their association with fetishism and the dark sides of sexuality are now commonplace in fashion shows. No one has done more to accelerate this movement than Jean Paul Gaultier, for whom sex is primarily fun.
(*Photos: Niall McInerney*)

TWO OUTFITS (*above*) from 'Nothing, by a Good-for-Nothing', his Spring-Summer 1987 women's collection which claimed 'personality first, only materials subsist'. Sparkling textures (*right*) from Gaultier's Autumn-Winter 1990–91 women's collection dedicated to 'past greatness and decadent elegance'.

'Everyone
my clothe
everybo
to bec
don't c
pre

2 EMBRYONIC ENFANT TERRIBLE

can wear
s but not
dy wants
use they
onform or
tect you'

IT WAS ON HIS EIGHTEENTH BIRTHDAY that Jean Paul Gaultier's big break came. Returning from school, he was met by his mother who told him that the house of Cardin had phoned – and that she had made an appointment for him to go in and discuss the drawings he had submitted. He was very excited, not, he claims, 'because I wanted to be famous. To be honest, I didn't want to be famous. What I wanted was to do. The two things are completely different. My goal was to do what I had admired for so long on television. Something very graphic and strong.'

As the day of the interview came nearer, he was, he admits, terrified. So much that he felt he just couldn't go alone. He persuaded his mother to come with him, but only as far as the building. There she left him and he was on his own. He went in, trembling with emotion, and there at the top of the stairs, waiting personally to receive him, as he thought, was Pierre Cardin himself. He seemed so elegant and refined and Jean Paul felt so big and clumsy that he was almost tongue-tied. He was so emotional about this meeting with one of the great *createurs* that he really saw nothing. He found it impossible to describe him later to his mother. 'Was he tall?' she asked. 'Slim?' He really had no idea. It is as if Cardin's aura had swallowed him in a glowing light. But he did remember his voice. It was very nasal but firm and had a unique intonation that Jean Paul was to get to know very well. At the time Gaultier was so confused, he could hardly understand what Cardin was saying. It went straight in one ear and out of the other. Even straight after the interview he could remember virtually nothing of the conversation – but he did realize that Cardin asked him when he could start work.

He had a job. At his first serious attempt, Jean Paul Gaultier's potential – it could hardly, at that stage, be called worth – had been recognized – and by a man whose abilities had made him a leading figure in the world of fashion, a man who could choose the best. Overawed as he was, Gaultier recalls that the interview ended on an absurd note. When he told Cardin that he was still at school but had certain times when he had no classes, the couturier said that there was no problem and it was agreed that he would work part-time in the afternoons. 'And', Cardin added, 'the pay will be 500 francs'. Overjoyed, confused, unable to think straight in all the excitement he was feeling, Jean Paul's jaw dropped in

ETHNIC BORROWINGS are frequently clichés of the catwalk, but in Gaultier's hands they are not tamed by Westernization. Instead he respects the integrity and beauty of the originals as aspects of strong indigenous cultures and uses them at full strength. To do otherwise is to patronize, as he is well aware. In his Winter 1994–95 collection 'The Long Journey' in which he visited Mongolia, Tibet, China and the far north for inspiration, he paid homage to Inuit civilization and the dwellers of the far north. The singer Björk was one of his models. (*Photos: Niall McInerney*)

‘We all wear American jeans, buy Chinese takeout. Food tells the whole story of how fashion is today’

amazement. '500 francs a day?' he asked. Cardin smiled austerely. 'No', he replied. 'A month'. It really didn't matter; Gaultier was so thrilled, he would probably have agreed to work for nothing.

Was Pierre Cardin a man of exceptional generosity or was he a man of vision? What was it he saw in the drawings of this rather raw suburban young man? Unlike most people who submitted fashion drawings, Gaultier had never formally studied fashion or design. He hadn't been to an art college. He was, in a sense, a totally untried commodity. Maybe that is what gave his work a freshness in Cardin's eyes. Gaultier looks back to the occasion with a certain amount of embarrassment. 'If I had known then what I know now, I would never have dared present such a portfolio,' he admits. 'It was so amateur. Having no confidence, I'd fallen into the trap of trying to show everything I could do. There was very little editing. My sketches contained a little bit of everything, including – most embarrassing of all – some old sequins I'd nicked from my grandmother and stuck onto the sketches.' He laughs. 'I mean, it was so tacky, I'd even used bits of gold paper for necklaces, bracelets and belts. Everything was in such disorder. Frankly, by the standards of couture, my designs were all very bad taste.'

Cardin was not the only couturier to respond to the unsolicited drawings, however. A week after seeing Cardin, Louis Feraud asked Gaultier to come and discuss his work. When Jean Paul was asked about his availability and he said that the only time he wasn't either at school or with Cardin was on Saturdays, the atmosphere changed dramatically. Angry at what he saw as a waste of his time, Feraud stood up and said frostily, 'As you're working for Cardin, you'd better just stay there.' Jean Paul was upset. He had gone to the interview innocent of the fact that fashion houses are suspicious, nervous places which demand total loyalty and discretion from employees. Nothing must be discussed outside the house. Everyone is treated as a potential spy. All other fashion houses are seen as threats and rivals. Ideas are sacrosanct and secrecy is all. The idea of a fledgling design assistant, privy to important decisions, flitting carelessly between houses, tittle-tattling like an eighteenth-century court cleric, was insupportable. It was a measure of Gaultier's gaucherie at this point that he had no idea of the diplomacy and etiquette of the fashion world, just as it was a measure of his innocence and openness that he assumed he could be trusted by

Decorative deliciousness – the flash of pattern, the richness of texture – has taken the place of volume and line, prerequisites of high fashion in the forties and fifties, as the way a couturier shows his strengths and gives his clothes their distinctive 'handwriting'. Gaultier's use of colour and surface detailing has made his one of the most instantly recognized of all Paris signatures.

These richly coloured jackets are from Jean Paul Gaultier's Autumn-Winter 1997–8 collection.
(Photos: Niall McInerney)

Big cats and the power of exotic furs have fascinated man since the Middle Ages. Even in modern imitation, the strength of fur has not diminished. In the past, on the backs of kings and emperors, it was about temporal power; today its charge is sexual, as in these two voluptuous examples from Gaultier's Winter 1994 collection, which took as its inspiration Rasputin and Tarras Bulba, and in an amalgam of names, was called 'Tarbullboud'deville'. (*Photos: Niall McInerney*)

'It's not funny to be

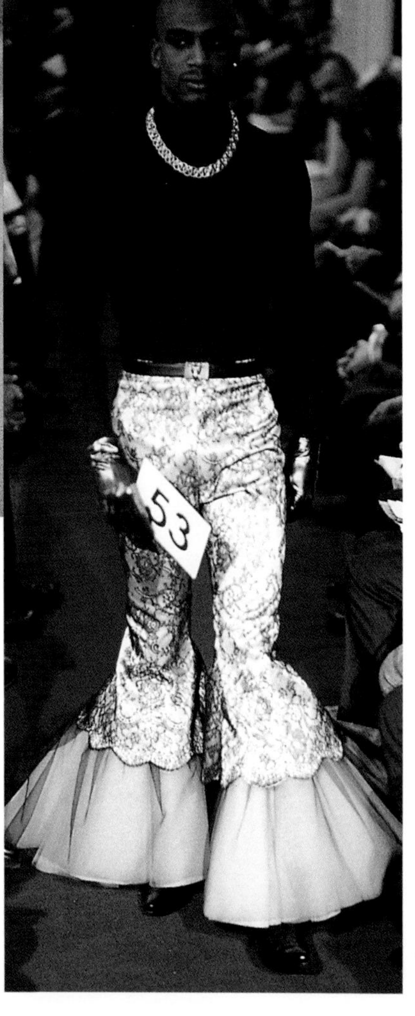

THE SINUOUS LINE breaking free in a froth of diaphanous material at the hemline has been a high-fashion cliché since the thirties. But in over sixty years, only Gaultier has seen fit to use the same semantics in dressing men. He expects us to be startled, amused and even briefly shocked but the question he is asking – why not? – hovers, awkwardly unanswerable, over the runway, exposing our preconceived attitudes to what is suitable for a woman and what a man may wear. (*Photos: Niall McInerney*)

different couturiers to do his work and keep his mouth shut. Although he now sees his design portfolios of those days as a slight embarrassment, they clearly contained enough for experienced couturiers to assess his worth. Both Cardin and Feraud were highly successful men of proven ability. That both liked his work says enough. But, to Gaultier's great surprise, he even heard from his hero, Yves Saint Laurent, to whom he had written more or less on the off-chance, enclosing some sketches. Although the house of Saint Laurent liked his sketches, they were worried about his taste levels and found his colours particularly unattractive. Normally, this would have dashed his fragile ego, but buoyed up by his success with Cardin, the criticism did not have such a dramatic effect, although it clearly troubled Gaultier that he had failed to impress the man he most admired in the fashion world. But he took comfort from being with Cardin, convinced that, with hard work, he would achieve his ambition to learn and know about fashion from an association with such a luminary on the international fashion scene. Above all, he was determined to develop the sort of good taste Saint Laurent talked of – but without sacrificing what he knew even at that stage was his uniquely original and lighthearted *esprit*.

Jean Paul Gaultier began with Cardin in April 1970. Academically, it was the worst possible time. He was supposed to be working for his Baccalaureate, in two months' time, but of course his head was full of the excitement of his new job and he could concentrate on nothing else. In his own words, he 'failed brilliantly, but I didn't give a stuff and my parents were forced to accept that Jean Paul and academic study had parted company'. He had enough to worry about building up his confidence at Cardin, where the design studio was full of young designers who could draw better than him and, to his eyes, seemed so sophisticated and *au courant* that he despaired of reaching their level. His feeling that, compared with them, he knew nothing about design, did nothing for his fragile ego.

a joke in France'

Surrounded by seemingly sophisticated worldly people, Jean Paul also felt at a disadvantage socially and artistically. Colleagues would talk about the latest Broadway show, discussing the stars as if they knew them, and he – as often as not – hadn't heard of any of them. There was also a great deal of jostling for the attention of Monsieur Cardin as he walked through the studio. Gauche, uncomfortable and feeling totally worthless, Gaultier would avoid catching Cardin's eye and even resorted to dropping a piece of paper on the floor so that he was hidden under the table retrieving it as the couturier walked by.

Today, when Cardin is no longer seen as being in the forefront of fashion, it is hard to imagine how revolutionary his approach was in the fifties and sixties, or how important his experiments with cut and fabric were considered. When, in 1963, he was given the first *Sunday Times* Fashion Award, he was praised for the fact that 'although many of his collections have been controversial, he remains true to his own inspiration'. It was an inspiration part oriental and part space-age and relied on precision of cut and an almost architectural purity of shape and scale. By the time Gaultier joined him he was no longer quite such a major name, having become involved in abstract ideas to an extent that practicality – and even wearability – became secondary.

Nevertheless, for Gaultier the Cardin experience was liberating. No longer creating imaginary collections in the manner of the great couturiers, he was finally helping – albeit in a very minor way – a great couturier create real clothes. At last he was in a fashion ambience, able to learn from his daily contacts

RICHLY PATTERNED and decorative materials have traditionally been used for female evening glamour. Gaultier annexes them for masculine fashion and gives them a practical, everyday application. His all-in-one jumpsuit sexily clings to the contours of the male figure, and the zip – for years something which high fashion felt must be kept hidden – is blatantly exposed, offering hints of sexual readiness and even aggression in this winter 1996 play on the tight-T-shirt syndrome of gay semantics.

Mayhem, paradox and parody are standard elements of Gaultier fashion presentations. He has used his catwalks to tell a story, invent a situation and present a mood with style and abandonment. This tableau came from his Spring-Summer 1986 collection, 'The Dolls' described in his press release as featuring 'the petticoat for all occasions'.
(Photo: Niall McInerney)

with creativity, and with just about every international fashion magazine in the world at his disposal. His fashion knowledge grew dramatically, as did his awareness of how globally all-encompassing the interests of a successful commercial fashion firm are. In this, of course, Cardin was exceptional, having used the sixties and the lustre of his name at that time, to build a vast network of licensees, making not just clothes but everything from perfume and socks to pots, pans and even plastic bowls, to sell under his label. It made him financially successful in a way no couturier had ever dreamed possible at that time, even though, eventually, it earned him the neglect and contempt of many in the fashion world.

Gaultier joined Cardin at the moment when the couturier was launching his venture into the arts, with his Paris theatre and exhibition complex L'Espace Pierre Cardin, and he found it not only exciting but liberating that a designer should wish to embrace exhibitions, restaurants and theatres as part of his overall fashion vision. For Jean Paul it put fashion at the centre of the cultural mix, which is exactly where it belongs. 'We were involved in designing things which had never previously been considered the concern of a fashion house,' he says. 'Plates, tapestries, even seats, were all designed in the Cardin studio. We were asked to come up with ideas for seats and I came up with an idea – but, you must realize, Studio Cardin was a place where anything goes; we could try any idea, it didn't matter if it seemed crazy – so I came up with the idea of a plastic seat – transparent – which would smoke slightly when people sat on it, the warmth of their bodies setting it off.'

It was not an idea taken up but, as Jean Paul says, 'It was the fact that I could even have such an idea which was so liberating. You could be as extravagant as you liked. In that house nothing frightened people. In fact, Cardin was such an amazingly original man, open to all ideas, that nothing ever seemed extravagant. I believed in him as the way forward. He had none of that awful French bourgeois narrowness. He was totally without prejudice. Everybody, including me, was allowed to give ideas. With Cardin, I always felt that anything was possible. He was very much the showman. He used to say, "I want to see a collection for women who go to the moon." Always, there was an idea. He worked in squares, circles and diagonals. He did many beautiful geometric shapes, although there were times when I asked myself, where is the woman?'

It was not a question he asked at his first real fashion show – the couture collection of July 1970. Although only a junior member of the team, Gaultier attended some of the fittings and was amazed at how quickly Cardin made decisions over highly complex cutting techniques and how sure he was of exactly what he wanted. The show itself was a revelation. Previously, Jean Paul had seen only 'highlights' on television. Here was the real thing, in its entirety. He found it so overwhelming that he cried. During the show, it was his very junior job to give the models

'Sometimes there is a show; sometimes there are clothes. I try to do both'

A COUTURE extravaganza from Gaultier's Spring-Summer 1998 collection which brings up to date the more theatrical of head-dresses from the golden age of Marie Antoinette and Versailles.

'I don't make works of art'

TRAINED IN THE traditional skills of couture, Gaultier can laugh at current ideas of glamour with the knowledge that his past gives him. The vulgarity of modern glitz is worlds away from the discreet opulence of the past and Gaultier loves to push it to the limit in order to reveal its very limitations. Marie Antoinette and the court of eighteenth-century Versailles would revel in the insanity of the clothes shown here, and there is no fear that their modern equivalents – today's fashion world – would miss the point of Gaultier's statement. For Spring 1992, 'Elegance Competition' accessories helped make the point.
(*Photos: Niall McInerney; drawings: Gladys Perint Palmer*)

A WILDLY ECLECTIC mixing of moods was the over-all characteristic of 'Travel Around the World in 168 Outfits' for the Spring-Summer 1989 collection. (*Photo: Niall McInerney*)

The lure of the harem and the exoticism of Eastern approaches to dress have exerted a powerful influence on the high-fashion glamour of the past ten years. Faces half hidden in many strands of exotic jewellery and heads swathed in extravagantly rich turbans have become standard items on the catwalks of the world. This beautiful example of the genre is from Gaultier's Spring-Summer 1998 collection, dedicated to Frida Kahlo, the Mexican painter and wife of Diego Rivera. *(Photo: Niall McInerney)*

their numbers but the whole thing went so fast and he was so much in a trance that he has no recall of getting beyond number one.

Eight months after joining Cardin, it was decided that the firm was overstaffed and, as he had been the last assistant appointed, Gaultier was made redundant. He went through an unsettled period after Cardin, working briefly with Jacques Esterel, whose fantasy ideas in the fifties and sixties had earned him the name of 'the court jester' of Paris fashion. It is interesting that in 1965, he pre-dated Gaultier's 'men in skirts' idea with a plaid kilted suit 'pour hommes' and he also experimented with another future Gaultier interest: pants with zippers back and front. He even wrote a song, as Gaultier was to do years later. Iconoclastic and fearlessly original in his heyday, Esterel refused to allow his designs to be constrained by preconceived concepts of taste or usage and it is obvious that, although

Like Ondine, the water sprite, she floats with strands of hair waving around her body in a *Midsummer Night's Dream* of innocence and sexuality, which for all the semi-nudity, has the purity of early morning mist hovering above an enchanted lake as dawn breaks. Or is she an Emperor's-new-clothes comment on the simplistic ideas which pass for fashion originality? As so often with Gaultier, there is no definitive answer. Subtlety and pluralism are at the root of his work and he is happy to raise questions which are not always immediately answerable, as here, in his collection for Summer 1993 called 'Classics Reviewed'. (*Photo: Niall McInerney*)

Jean Paul was with him only a matter of months, the young man absorbed much from the older man which was to become part of his own fashion philosophy. Looking back, Gaultier doesn't recall his time at Esterel as being enjoyable, however. It was only three years before Esterel's death and, in Jean Paul's eyes, he was a man who had lost his flair and wit. But it was a much smaller business than Cardin's and this helped Gaultier's confidence – as did wearing clothes from Esterel's menswear range. After a few months, he was made redundant again.

A brief and unhappy period in the style agency Cincept, churning out forecast designs for the rag trade, left Gaultier frustrated and demoralized. He had tried twice to get into the Dior design studio but had failed because Marc Bohan felt his work to be too reminiscent of Cardin's very strong fashion signature. His work in the agency forced him to think hard about what it was he wanted out of a fashion career. Did he want to spend his life making hundreds of sketches per week, knowing that he would never see them made into clothes? He knew the answer. His heart was still in couture. Hearing that the house of Patou was looking for a design assistant, he applied for and, to his great delight, was given the job even though it meant a dramatic drop in salary.

The fashion house founded in 1919 by Jean Patou was famous in the twenties and early thirties for creative clothes for 'the modern woman who leads an active life', as Patou put it. His genius lay in his skill in assessing the way in which women's lives were becoming much less structured and constrained and then producing clothes to fit into their changing lifestyles. His attitudes towards dress were very similar to those of his arch rival, Chanel. The fact that she hated him so much that she became furiously jealous if his work appeared anywhere near hers in *Vogue* gives an indication of his abilities: Chanel only loathed those who threatened her by being almost as good. Since Patou's death in 1936, the house had existed mainly on the proceeds of 'Joy', the most expensive perfume in the world and, after World War II, had employed various designers, including Marc Bohan and Karl Lagerfeld. When Gaultier joined, the design director was Michel Goma, who had held the appointment since 1963.

Gaultier was thrilled to be back in what he saw as his true milieu,

IS THERE ANY REASON why a man shouldn't wear feathers? Does maribou compromise musculinity? Is strong colour unsuitable for male dress? Not in Jean Paul Gaultier's book. His philosophy of fashion is truly egalitarian: what is fashion sauce for the gander is certainly sauce for the geese in his opinion, as he proudly shows in this example from 'Latin Lovers of the Forties' his Spring-Summer 1995 menswear show 'for men who will nick their girlfriends' dresses'. (*Photo: Niall McInerney*)

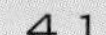

WAFTING, WHISPERING in drifts of semi-diaphanous layers over delicate fabrics, modern fashion is both more subtle and more complex than much of the high style of the past. Today, there is a lightness and fragility, a multifaceted movement as different fabrics and materials are used to work with and against the body, both revealing and concealing in the change of a second. (*Photos: Niall McInerney*)

'My clothes are lifted from life itself'

Wildly shaggy and shapeless furs and feathers – imitation or real – have long been considered tacky, but Jean Paul Gaultier enjoys taking what many consider bad-taste looks and transforming them into stylish high fashion. (*Photos: Niall McInerney*)

living once again the *Falbalas* fantasy of an haute couture fashion house, including, this time, the intrigue and jealousies he had been largely unaware of in his inexperienced days with Pierre Cardin. Patou was a true couture establishment, as old-fashioned and venerable as the building in rue St Florentin which had been its headquarters since 1922. Jean Paul loved the romance of its elegant, high-ceilinged salons but he soon realized that most of the attitudes found there were as Old World as the building. It was a house living in the past in every sense but, for Gaultier, that was all part of the charm. He was fascinated by the workrooms, dedicated to the most delicate and time-consuming methods of working, where hand-made and embroidered dresses could monopolize workers for as long as two months, and where the traditions of the grand couturiers of the thirties still pertained. Jean Paul remembers how respectfully everyone treated the clothes, as if they were precious artefacts, and with what love they were taken from hangers, placed on the models and then, equally carefully, replaced on the hangers. Clothes were never piled on a table or thrown over a chair, even *pro tem*, at Patou.

Feathers currently define high glamour and few creators use them to such dramatic effect as Gaultier. This feather bolero from his Spring-Summer collection for 1997 was worn by the Israeli transsexual singer Dana International, on the triumphant night when she won the 1998 Eurovision Song Contest. Its magnificence lived up to the drama of the occasion. (*Photos: Niall McInerney*)

In such a world, Gaultier flourished – but only up to a point. He admits, 'It wasn't as much fun as working for Pierre Cardin.' He liked and respected Goma, although he didn't always agree with his design decisions. But he was less happy with the hypocrisy and intrigue. Eighteen months after he joined the firm there was a palace revolution at Patou; Goma left and his place was taken by Angelo Tarlazzi, who had formerly been one of his assistants. With the change came a new mood which Gaultier felt was at variance with the original spirit of Patou that Goma had tried to perpetuate. Whereas he and Goma had often disagreed about design questions, they had usually understood each other, and both had shown sufficient respect for the other's opinion to try to find a compromise. Under the new director, that didn't happen. As his designs were increasingly set aside, Gaultier became frustrated and moody. Slowly, his initial enthusiasm for the house of Patou evaporated. He knew that he could not continue there.

Looking back over his early career, Gaultier remembers certain key moments which have affected his entire design life and which were undoubtedly responsible for making him the sort of designer he now is.

One of them goes back to his time at Cardin when, after a show, a woman came backstage to congratulate the couturier. To Jean Paul, used to the strength of Cardin's clothes, based on his belief that all fashion must begin with an intellectual idea, the woman's appearance, although elegant, seemed so understated as to almost be *triste*. 'It was very austere, but very strong,' he recalls. 'She was dressed in khaki. A crepe de chine shirt and trousers cut like a man's. She looked sombre and yet I was very conscious of the difference between the fashion philosophy of her creator – it was, of course, Yves Saint Laurent – and that followed by us at Cardin. I was really upset and perplexed and I spent a long time analysing it. Eventually, I understood. What Saint Laurent had done was create beautiful clothes that revealed the individual. You saw the *woman*, not her couturier. It was then I realized that gadgets, ideas and complicated detailing aren't what make good clothes. It is balance, not ideas, which make clothes – and women – beautiful.'

It was a seminal moment. If, as he has since claimed of Cardin, 'he taught me everything', it was the experience of Yves Saint Laurent which made Gaultier really question the role of the couturier *vis-a-vis* his customer, the woman. As he was to say in an interview many years later, 'I want to design for women as they are…women have traumatized themselves for the past twenty years, often spoiled their health and frazzled their nerves for a physical ideal which really doesn't have anything to do with true style.'

While at Patou, Jean Paul Gaultier first came across the inherent fascism which used to linger, unspoken and therefore unquestioned, beneath the grandeur of an old-style *maison de couture*. 'In any fashion show,' he says, 'the model plays a crucial role. It is vital to choose the right one for the mood of the times as well as the mood of the collection. My ideas of what I want in a model were influenced by my time at Patou, which was, I now realize, a very conservative house. From the attitudes at Patou, I found out what I didn't want and, therefore, found out what I *did* want.' He remembers talking about a very beautiful model whom he thought would be marvellous for a Patou show. She was not only beautiful, she was black and in 1971 the idea of a Paris fashion house using a black model was considered shocking. It wasn't that people felt it

Pastoral delicacy and the simple elegance of the bucolic are not often evoked in the hothouse atmosphere of the Paris fashion houses. Here Gaultier shows cut-out leaves which suggested a country idyll, on apparently unsophisticated shapes. For Spring-Summer 1991, 'The Couple – Adam and Eve of Today, Rastas', Gaultier, for the first time presented a collection 'reassembling men and women together, with a general image of masculinity and femininity in agreement and disagreement'. (*Photo: Niall McInerney*)

impossible for a black woman to convey the *esprit* of French fashion. It was much more basic – and to Jean Paul, more sinister. The response to his suggestion was final: 'Are you mad? We could never do that. The Americans would be horrified – and then where would sales be?' As he says, 'I was deeply shocked at such an absurd attitude and I made up my mind that if I were ever in a position to make such decisions I would never take that view.'

The spirit of French fashion in the early seventies was much the same as it was in London at the time, where youth had come in on a rollercoaster race around Carnaby Street and the King's Road to find the perfect personification of the new mood in fashion. Jean Shrimpton – beautiful but rather flat-chested – and Twiggy – beautiful but totally flat-chested – had given birth to a new fashion ideal: the boyish, flat-as-a-board woman with long legs and no hips. Every model in the world felt she had to comply. The absurdity of subscribing to one idea of perfection was brought home to Gaultier at Patou one day when he came across a model binding her breasts flat with tape. When he asked her why she was doing it, he was stunned by her answer. 'They won't use me if I have a figure. And I need the work.' He was appalled at such narrowness.

It was at Patou that Gaultier met the woman who was to have a deeper and more lasting influence on him than any of the designers with whom he worked. Anna Pawlovski came into Gaultier's life in 1972. An Oriental-looking beauty, with her black hair cut in a Louise Brooks twenties-style fringe, she was strikingly different from most models at that time, although in a strong Parisian tradition: exotic models with Far-Eastern looks were nothing new. Dior and Yves Saint Laurent, for example, had both used Eurasian models. Jean Paul had an instant rapport with Anna, based on a shared sense of humour and, perhaps, a slight feeling of standing apart and outside the hothouse circle of haute couture. His enthusiasm for her looks was shared by Tarlazzi and she became a model for Patou.

The early seventies were years of learning for Gaultier – about himself and life, as well as fashion. Like most homosexuals, he had been aware of his orientation since puberty but, unlike many, he had accepted it with no apparent trauma. He now feels that his grandmother had divined his

'The line between masculinity and femininity can be a very troubled frontier'

THERE IS A world of difference between the runway high jinks which many designers, including Gaultier, give us and the total mastery of fabric which is the province of the master. With the possible exception of Yves Saint Laurent, no-one in Paris can beat Gaultier at tailoring. With his sophisticated eye, he is able to work within masculine tailoring traditions to produce a high fashion stylishness with the minimum of adaptation. From his Winter 1998–9 couture collection. *(Photos: Niall McInerney)*

'In France, we are paralyzed by chic'

ONE OF THE things which makes Gaultier's such a strongly individual voice is his ability to cross fashion borders with total authority. For many seasons he has explored the juxtaposition of the *soignée* and simple to produce his own brand of high fashion sophistication, as he does here with the solidity of knitwear and sheerness of silk – although, of course, the knitwear in question is gossamer-light and in no way threatens the delicate balance between fabrics which is an essential of the well-designed creation. From his Winter 1998–9 couture collection. *(Photo: Niall McInerney)*

true sexuality – not difficult, observing his interests in almost exclusively feminine concerns when he stayed with her – and had tried to lead him to its acceptance. He remembers vividly how she gave him a book to read when he was quite young which contained a homosexual character attracted to Moroccan boys. It was a strange act in what even she would have to accept was a strange upbringing and, when he had read the book, she said, 'You see, this man is suffering from a sickness but that doesn't mean to say that he isn't nice. If you see a man suffering like him you should be nice to him.' When he tells this tale, Gaultier grins roguishly and adds, 'She didn't guess how nice I could be!'

Nevertheless, Jean Paul's sexuality, although never in doubt – 'When I went to the film of *Romeo and Juliet*, it was Romeo not Juliet I dreamed of, night after night' – was not as strong a preoccupation as fashion, and it wasn't until he was twenty that he had his first gay experience which was, as he succinctly puts it, 'very bad'. Before that, when he was seventeen, his mother had talked about him meeting someone for whom he cared. When he said, 'What if it isn't a woman?', she had replied that, 'if two people really love each other, that is all that matters'.

As he began to make a reasonable but certainly not handsome living, Jean Paul's obsessive interest in British and American pop music made him feel that he should, at least, visit London – to travel to New York in the early seventies was much more than his budget could stand. In any case, the pop stars who really excited him were British. Inevitably, he responded to the androgynous appeal of David Bowie and the sexual omnivorousness of Mick Jagger and the Rolling Stones. The unisex dressing of many British pop stars perfectly fitted his attitudes and he wore lace shirts and velvet with all the decadent flair of a French Gary Glitter, although looking back now, he says that most of his clothes came from flea markets. 'To be honest', he adds, 'I've never dressed fashionably. And I never made any clothes for myself. But I've always admired men with the courage to dress in a way that other men are afraid of.'

From the beginning, when he only had enough money to visit London once or twice a year, he fell in love, not just with the city, but also with the attitude of the people, especially the young. 'I find the French very snobby,' he confesses. 'They're not friendly and their attitudes are, in my view, frequently negative. I think it is very difficult to be young in France, whereas in England, the young bring fun to the streets. There is a sense of freedom and strength that I don't find on the streets of Paris. And energy! The French are too bourgeois and conformist.' As he told John Duka of *Interview* in 1986, 'I feel closer to the streets of London than the streets of Paris because I hate the poorness of Paris streets. By "poor" I mean not rich in imagination. Everybody wants to be like the other one… they want to be anonymous. In London, I don't really get my inspiration. I get my energy.'

Certainly, in the early seventies, Gaultier thought quite seriously of moving to London. He had managed to sell some design ideas to Quorum and felt sure that he could make a living. 'But, at that time, I had a boyfriend in Paris,' he says. 'And so it wasn't the time. I thought, "Later…", but it never happened. Not that I have any regrets. I love London and I always have fun there. It's not always easy to have fun in the city where you work.' Quite apart from that, as Lionel Vermeil, his press officer of almost twenty years' standing, says of Gaultier and his unique fashion approach, 'For Jean Paul, in any collection, the most important thing is the mix and it has three parts. First, of course, is sex and his obsession with having us all be honest about it. Second, is his belief in the intermixing of ethnic strands to make a complete whole. And third, is Paris. Jean Paul is *very* French. He sees the faults in French society but that doesn't mean he's not a Frenchman. Actually, what he is is a Parisian – and that's what affects everything he is doing.'

'There is no age in my clothes'

WHAT MIGHT be called the witty transfer has always appealed to Gaultier's puckish sense of humour. Here he takes the feeling of a classic trenchcoat and turns it into a swimming costume – the obvious link that both are created in response to water gives the borrowing a very Gaultier slant. From his Spring-Summer 2000 couture collection. *(Photo: Niall McInerney)*

'My f
a
pro
stron
charac
outs

3 SOMETIME INNOCENT ABROAD

ashion is
lot about
jecting a
unique
er to the
de world

THE FASHION BUSINESS REWARDS successful designers with obscene largesse. Even the many second-rate talents who get to the top – aided and abetted by partners who are first-rate businessmen – can become millionaires in less than a dozen years. But such generosity has its flipside. The fashion world is both hard and cynical towards aspirants. Young designers rarely find it easy to make their mark. For every genius – and, as with every other creative field, there are many fewer than PRs and journalists would have us believe – who, like Yves Saint Laurent, enters a firm and is offered the job of creative director at the age of twenty-one, there are many hundreds who wait much longer to be recognized.

And, while waiting, they take what jobs they can in order to keep in the swim as much as to keep afloat. Jean Paul Gaultier was no exception. He worked at many different levels before he was in the position to create collections under his own name. Much that he undertook was repetitive and boring. His work at the style bureau, Cincept, could involve whole days in coming up with variations on the theme of pockets or collars. Boring hack work, it carried with it a sense of doom and futility because, to a designer, the drawing is merely a step towards the physical realization of a creation whereas, to the style predictor it is, by necessity, a sterile end in itself – what drawings are translated into fabric are never done so under his supervision. Rather like removing a child from a mother, it robs the true fashion designer of the point of his experience.

Jean Paul Gaultier hated the style bureau but did not find being a freelance designer necessarily frustrating. He produced designs for the ready-to-wear labels Yves Delorme and Philippe Lelong. His first collection, which he created for Paul Rottenberg Vison, was of furs. Such work tided him over and gave him a very different perspective and experience from those he had had in his work with couture houses. The two fashion strands came together in 1974 when he began working for Cardin again. The Cardin empire stretched across the world, and Gaultier's new contract for a year was with Cardin-Philippines, where he was to work as a stylist and also supervise manufacture of a ready-to-wear range made there for the American market. Such convoluted paths are common in the fashion world where the search for cheap labour forces even the grandest names in the fashion capitals of Paris, New York and

THE SPIRIT OF saucy seaside postcards is often caught by Jean Paul Gaultier in his sailorboy suits which appeal to him as much for their nautical associations as for their strongly linear design impact. He knows that naval dress is strong enough to take a certain amount of satirical fun. The above ensemble is from his Spring-Summer 1989 collection as is the illustration near right. The outfit on the far right was from the Spring 1991 collection. (*Photo: Niall McInerney; drawings: Gladys Perint Palmer*)

From Gaultier's Spring-Summer 1997 mensw‿ar collection, entitled 'House of Pleasure'.
(Photo: Niall McInerney)

THE WELL-BUILT sailor out for a night on the town has become not only a standard piece of port mythology but also a staple of gay iconography – a fact played up by Gaultier in his sparkly matelot (*far left*) although he also shows the simple elegance of real naval gear as a relaxed way for landlubbers to dress down (*near left*) in the macho pin-up, sailor version from 'Pin-Up Boys', Spring-Summer 1996. (*Photo: Niall McInerney; drawing: Tom of Finland*)

Milan to crisscross the globe in order to maintain the winning formula of low costs and high profits.

It was the first time Jean Paul had left his parents for any length of time and he was nervous. It was a job demanding much more than designing clothes. He would be making decisions at many different levels and – much more difficult for a man still basically very shy – he would have to have a public profile as the official 'face' of Cardin in Manila. He decided to travel via India and Nepal, meeting up with friends he'd made in Paris. He arrived in Calcutta, that teeming, seething city of overcrowded humanity, and was appalled. But he was also delighted by the marvellous colour sense of Indian women and the dignity of their bearing. He was fascinated by the delicate intricacy of Indian jewellery and silverwork. But it was Nepal which he really enjoyed, finding the people *sympatique* and the country beautiful. It was the beginning of his life-long respect for ethnic approaches to design and decoration.

Jean Paul Gaultier's arrival in Manila was inauspicious. After an exhausting journey, he found that his accommodation was a sordid room above the shop. It was the worst possible introduction to what he could see would be a difficult year. He tried to make the best of things and managed to be positive and cheerful for newspaper reporters, one of whom described him as 'six feet, twenty-two years, with carrot-coloured hair if somewhat bleached by the sun, charming French accent and oozing with Gallic appeal'. The copy went on to claim that he had fallen in love with the country and quoted Gaultier's enthusiastic comments: 'It is fantastic! If I want to have French food tonight, I can. Tomorrow I can go Chinese. The next night I can have Spanish, and so on.'

Very little else pleased him. He found the taste level of the women with whom he dealt abominably low and believed that everyone had sold out to the worst aspects of American culture. Of the many rich women he fitted for clothes, he now wonders if one of them was Mrs Marcos. If so, it could explain the difficulty he would ultimately have in leaving the Philippines, because although he was desperately unhappy and disorientated, the rich women of Manila loved his clothes, considered that he was bringing them true Parisian haute couture and were devastated at the thought that he could abandon them.

No couturier has the mastery of kitch and camp that Gaultier has. His deliberate exercises in the gaucherie of bad taste never fail to delight the audience at his shows, and everyone was amused by this sweet pair who paraded together in 'The Couple', his collection for Spring-Summer 1991, Gaultier's exercise in unisex and androgenous looks. (*Photo: Niall McInerney*)

THE SEMIOTICS OF uniform are to do with power and masculine bonding, as Gaultier is well aware. But he raises his own quizical eyebrow and subverts the whole thing by introducing the figure on the far left in a classic piece of Gaultier debunking of the clichés we are all happy to cling to. (*Photo: Niall McInerney*)

A brief visit from his friend Anna, who had recently been appointed as a model at Yves Saint Laurent, brought his unhappiness to a head. Her presence made him realize how homesick he was, not just for friends and family, not just for Europe and France but, above all, for Paris and its vibrant fashion scene. He was determined to return. His decision met with concerted opposition, unofficially and officially. Even when he pretended that he would only be leaving the country for a short while to visit a fabric fair in France, he could not obtain a leaving permit. Desperate, he tried going to the airport without any warning. To his horror and amazement, officials turned him back on the pretext that he had been blacklisted. When he asked why, he discovered the peculiar logic that operates in dictatorships. Nobody could answer his questions. All that he could get in the way of an answer was that if he was blacklisted then he *had* to have

IN ONE OF THE MOST accomplished pieces of trompe l'oeil embroidery to be seen on a Paris runway, Gaultier acknowledges the eternal lure of the big cat and makes a dress of stunning power and style for Autumn-Winter 1997–8, dedicated to female power. The workmanship is so superb that, for a moment at least, it could almost be the real thing.
(Photos: Niall McInerney)

'My favourite period is the fifties. Femininity was more exaggerated then'

done something wrong and he must know what it was. Homosexuals are not liked in dictatorships. It is possible that Gaultier had been under surveillance and his behaviour had displeased the authorities – but it is much more likely, if this were the case, that the authorities would wish to be rid of him. Gaultier's view that he was the victim of selfish women married to influential officials is almost certainly the correct one.

Desperation made him ingenious. He asked his mother to send him a telegram, pretending that his grandmother had died. It was agreed that he should return to France for the funeral – but the licensees who owned the Cardin-Philippines rights refused to pay for his ticket as they claimed that he had broken his contract. Even then, when he again went to the airport, his departure was delayed while the immigration officials checked and, as is the way in dictatorships, double-checked that he was allowed to go. Only then was his passport stamped.

Jean Paul Gaultier arrived back in Paris in July 1975, determined to use all the experiences of the last few years to create for himself a true place in French fashion. By chance, he met his oldest friend, Donald Potard, who had been at school with him. Through him, he was introduced to Francis Menuge, the man whom Gaultier has described as the love of his life. Although not centrally involved in fashion, Menuge was interested in making modern jewellery, using not only materials but also techniques not even considered by the more traditional craftsmen. He was greatly excited by electronics and wanted to explore the possibilities of creating a range of luminous jewellery.

It was in essence an idea out of its time. It would have appealed to people in the sixties and even, perhaps, in the eighties but, for the laid-back, pot-smoking seventies it was too high-tech. At a time when things

LIKE MANY DESIGNERS in Paris, Gaultier often conjures hints of the *Belle Epoque*, but in his case always seen with very modern eyes. Gaultier never slips into pastiche because he uses the past merely as a jumping-off point for the present. Here, an hourglass evening gown is made totally up-to-date in denim and feathers. From his Spring-Summer 1998–9 couture collection.
(*Photo: Niall McInerney*)

'natural', whether contrived by Laura Ashley or nothing more than ripped and shredded Levis, along with things 'ethnic', usually a bastardized mix of Indian cotton and embroidered Mongolian lambskin coats, were what the young favoured, and jewellery was reduced to rows of brightly coloured hand-strung beads, which could be created in an afternoon over a bottle of wine and a joint, urban slickness was not required. Even though the luminous jewellery was featured in important magazines like *Paris Match* and *Depêche Mode*, no one would put it into production.

In fact, it wasn't just the jewellery idea which was out of its time. So was the design approach of Jean Paul Gaultier. His belief that the basis of all true fashion was French couture had been out of date even in the late sixties. By 1975, it was dangerously out of touch with what was happening in fashion. Paradoxically, it was Gaultier's hero, Yves Saint Laurent, who had seen the future even when his house was considered the *ne plus ultra* of Paris couture. As far back as 1960, his Left Bank collection, attempting to reflect the values of the Beat generation and the attitudes of the Existentialists, had introduced influences from the streets. It had been the excuse for the house of Dior to sack him. In 1968, he had been deeply moved by the student street fighters who came out in favour of the workers, rioting against government policies, and turned Boulevard Saint Germain into a battleground. As a sign of his solidarity he produced a sombre black collection with ethnic headbands and fringes as well as the ubiquitous student duffel coat. And wasn't it Yves Saint Laurent who announced in 1971 that couture was decadent and dead and he would have no more of it? Even though he quietly back-tracked two years later and reintroduced it, his proclamation had made the point: in future, the vibrancy of fashion would be engendered by ready-to-wear.

Jean Paul Gaultier was not so foolish nor so out of touch to be unaware that seventies fashion was undergoing change. He was no Canute, either. He knew perfectly well that the privileged world of couture was out of step with world developments. But, initially at least, when he returned from the Philippines, he had difficulty in grasping the implications of what was, unquestionably, the most cataclysmic period of change in the twentieth century. He now admits, 'It's true that when I came back to Paris I was so happy and relieved that, to begin with, I didn't want to question anything. Of course, I was aware of the changes that were taking place. Everything was being questioned. But I knew that I could – and I would – be able to use my couture experience and my knowledge of ready-to-wear in order to do something not just totally modern but uniquely Jean Paul Gaultier.'

He worked at his ideas by drawing – just as he had when he had produced his teenage 'collections' in the manner of the current couturiers. But this time his ideas were focused – not on pastiche of the creations of the great names of fashion but on what Jean Paul Gaultier felt that fashion in the mid-seventies was about and could be in the future. He and Menuge were interested in the *Createurs-Industriels* movement, set up by Andree Putman and Didier Grumbach in 1972. They had high hopes of obtaining backing from the organization, which had already helped designers like Castelbajac and Miyake. That didn't happen but, although it was devastating at the time, it didn't really matter. The important outcome of the work Gaultier produced to present to *Createurs-Industriels* was the dossier of designs he presented.

THE GAULTIER MAN is strong and confident. That is why he can have fun with his appearance. The designer sees no reason why men shouldn't glitter, adorn themselves in fur or wear a suit as an all-in-one. As these pictures show, he is quite right, but for those not entirely convinced he can take something as conventional as metelot stripes and make an equally strong statement with them.

THE ENSEMBLES ON the facing page were taken from the Autumn-Winter 1990–91 collection called 'Les Pieds Nickeles', an homage to French comic strip characters. On this page, are outfits from (*left*) 'The Fanatics of Photography', Autumn-Winter 1992–3 collection, and the 'Latin Lover of the Forties', Spring-Summer 1995 collection (*above*).
(*Photos: Niall McInerney*)

He claimed to have worked harder on that project than he had ever done in his life. It really made him think not only of fashion but of what he meant by fashion. Avoiding making designs which had any obvious commercial application, he radically examined what he knew about fashion and then used that analysis to project his own view of modern fashion. And, of course, he was sufficiently sophisticated to realize that clothes are only a part of fashion and that true fashion is part of a cultural movement which includes all aspects of society, from the way people dress on the streets to what films they see and what food they eat. As he told *Women's Wear Daily* in 1984, 'Everything that passes before my eyes is turned into a fashion reflex. My passions are largely visual.'

Jean Paul Gaultier's great strength was his experience and knowledge of a world outside the confines of Paris fashion, along with cultural interests considerably broader that those in many French fashion houses. As he has said, 'I find the majority of French designers tend to sleep away on their big pillows, saying "Oh, yes, that's so beautiful", "Vive le chic Parisien", "Chic is everything". Paris wants entirely too much to be chic.' His fashion antennae have always been widely tuned: to Poiret and Sonia

GAULTIER IS generally known for his attempts to put men in skirts. He has tried to show that it is only sexual stereotypes which assume that men lose their masculinity if they are wearing skirts rather than trousers. The fact is that Gaultier is far ahead of most of us but he is confident that in time the logic of his attitude will become accepted. Above, from Spring-Summer 1995 and right, from Autumn-Winter 1994–5.
(*Photos: Niall McInerney*)

Delaunay as much as to Ossie Clark or Bill Gibb. Misia Sert and the Marchesa Casati were names as familiar to him as those of Jerry Hall or Marie Helvin. He was aware of Alice Cooper and Roxy Music; *Clockwork Orange* and Allen Jones. In other words, he had the social, sexual and creative pulse of the moment. What if Andree Putman did reject his ideas? Preparing them had been the important step forward that he required. He knew what he stood for as a designer. He had, in fact, evolved his fashion philosophy, although he would have found the term inappropriately pompous at the time. He explained it clearly in an interview with *Blitz* when he said, 'Of course, I'm influenced by the street but it's about the way people behave; movies, music, everything…I take in all these images, mix them up and then the ideas come out.'

There was only one thing for it. Although he was making a reasonable living from freelance work, designing for ready-to-wear manufacturers like Mayagor, doing swimwear for Anabel and furs for Chombert, Gaultier knew that the moment had come. He must become a designer in his own right. The year was 1976. Francis Menuge and Donald Potard agreed entirely that the time was right. The problem with which they were faced was simple: none of them had enough money to set up a firm. Jean Paul was desperate to have a show. He knew he couldn't produce a full collection but, surely, one show…? As he recalls it, 'France is not like England. The spirit isn't free as it is in London where you're not ashamed to sell your clothes in Portobello Road. In Paris, you have to look serious. If you don't look professional, they treat you like a joke.'

Jean Paul's first collection under his own name was presented to the world in October 1976. He had scraped up enough money to put on a show which he now describes as 'an upholsterer's collection' because, using materials he could find – and afford – in markets, he picked up reproduction tapestries; a kind of braided straw and some wild silk from India. He now looks back and says, 'That first show was terrible. We only had a few patterns and everything else was variations. At the time, fashion was very loose so, imagining I could repeat the success of Dior's New Look, I made everything very tight. It was a terrible flop.'

Everything was done on a shoestring and nobody was paid. Anna Pawlovski persuaded her friends to model. The chief hairdresser at

'I've always tried to balance the eccentric and the classic'

Alexandre did their hair. Lots of press files were prepared. Jean Paul's friends looking after the press chose the time of the show very carefully, picking an important slot only to find that Emmanuelle Khanh, at that time a major figure in Paris fashion, was showing at the same time. All important journalists went to her show, leaving Gaultier with 'the oldest journalists in the world. All French. The ones who hadn't been invited to Emmanuelle Khanh. They sat in the front row, feeling important for the first time in their lives and expecting cocktails afterwards – not that we had any money for that'. But it wasn't entirely a fiasco. The room was full, even if most of the audience *were* gatecrashers. The audience was enthusiastic. Gaultier even received a few brief mentions in *Le Monde* and *Figaro*, and he actually sold a shirt in a boutique called Victoire, but the concierge who sewed for him in her spare time was charging so much that he made a loss. Although he now calls it 'a muddle of a collection', Jean Paul had begun. And he was determined to continue. Muddle or not, the Jean Paul Gaultier of the future was there, even if only in embryo, in the form of a studded leather jacket worn with a tutu which revealed the navel. The outfit was worn with tennis shoes – a revolutionary statement in Paris fashion at that time.

For his second show, Gaultier took over a café-theatre called La Course des Miracles and invited people for a meal. The theme of the

'My fashion is a lot about projecting a strong, unique character to the outside world'

collection was loosely based on Robin Hood. He eked out the show by using some of the furs he had designed for Chombert and one or two models from the collection he had done for Mayagor. It had its moments of theatre of the absurd, not least when, in the dark, nobody could find the shoes for the models and they had to go out without them. Half the audience laughed and the other half seemed more interested in a little hat bought in Hong Kong than anything designed by Gaultier.

By dint of selling drawings to ready-to-wear manufacturers all round Paris, eating spaghetti or visiting Jean Paul's parents for meals and even sleeping on friends' floors, it seemed that enough money might be amassed to make a third show a possibility. It was held in the Theatre des Champs-Elysées in October 1977, made possible by a financial tie-in with a ready-to-wear company called Berthe Moline for whom Gaultier would create a collection in return for a cash injection. Nineteen models were hired, at a cost of 600 francs each and a dress of their choice. Professional help was available. And then, less than ten days before the show, the backer withdrew. From that point, as Gaultier admits, it became a nightmare. Even his relationship with Anna began to sour. She had become an important model, one of French fashion's personalities. She was not being paid and by appearing in Gaultier's show she was bestowing considerable cachet. She felt she was being taken advantage of. All of this, Gaultier could rationalize but he was haunted by insecurities; perhaps the atmosphere was bad because, finding his clothes not good enough, she regretted an involvement which could compromise her professionally? Certainly, the atmosphere was tainted by misunderstanding – that is, until the show. Then everything cleared because, although Gaultier still

FASHION DESIGNERS have long realized that there are no stereotypes in beauty. In this they have generally been ahead of most people. The runways of the fashion capitals are hosts to models from virtually every corner of the world, but few designers fit the face and the fashion with as much tact and delicacy as Gaultier does in his attempts to show (as these pictures confirm) that beauty, in clothes or features, is not confined to any group or civilization. The ensemble on the left is from 'Cyberbaba', Spring-Summer 1996, for the woman who 'on her travels, borrows different elements here and there'. The outfit on the right is from a 1997–98 collection. (*Photos: Niall McInerney*)

Not all floral patterns are whimsical, lady-like and tame. Strong colours, simple shapes and powerful patterns can make them zing with glamour and richness. Add a touch of glitter and you have a look capable of appealing to the most sophisticated, as Gaultier proves here with two examples from Spring-Summer 1993, 'Classics Reviewed'.
(*Photos: Niall McInerney*)

received very little press coverage, his unique ability to mix materials, question the canons of taste and make exciting juxtapositions of ethnic elements and traditional Parisian chic were beginning to make it clear to the fashion *cognoscenti* that an original new talent was emerging. The aficionados – growing in number with each show – began to talk, and those who hadn't previously shown any interest – not least the French press – decided that they, too, needed to keep an eye on Gaultier.

But it wasn't really until his fourth collection that people began to seriously talk about the new boy on the scene. In the interim, he had appeared in *Marie-Claire*, probably the one French magazine which championed his work early and consistently; in *Jardin des Modes* and various Paris newspapers. There was a feeling of hope in the Gaultier camp, but still no money. The show was kept simple, graphic and very strong, a statement in black and white. The audience was enthusiastic. There were hordes of young Gaultier groupies. It was an exciting, even triumphant time – or could have been. There was one snag. The Gaultier show was scheduled at the same time as Saint Laurent's fur presentation. Although journalists from *Elle* and *Marie-Claire* appeared, most of the senior magazine editors were at Saint Laurent, following an unbreakable convention which states that wealthy houses with large budgets have to be wooed by a magazine's top personnel. That means being prominently seen at the show. By giving a public vote of confidence in that way, the magazine is assured of the advertising revenue without which it cannot exist. It happened then. It does today. No matter how intriguing the talk of Gaultier's exciting new ideas, he had no advertising budget, so there was no question: the international fashion power was sitting in the front row of Saint Laurent.

Gaultier accepted this as a fact of life in fashion. He understood its inevitability. But that didn't change the situation: after four collections – each stronger and more original than the last – although an individual handwriting had clearly emerged, there was nothing left with which to write. His only hope was to borrow money. He turned to Philippe Lelong, a manufacturer who specialized in the Arab market and for whom Gaultier had been providing sketches for the past two years, at a very promising rate per sketch. Pretending that things were going so well that

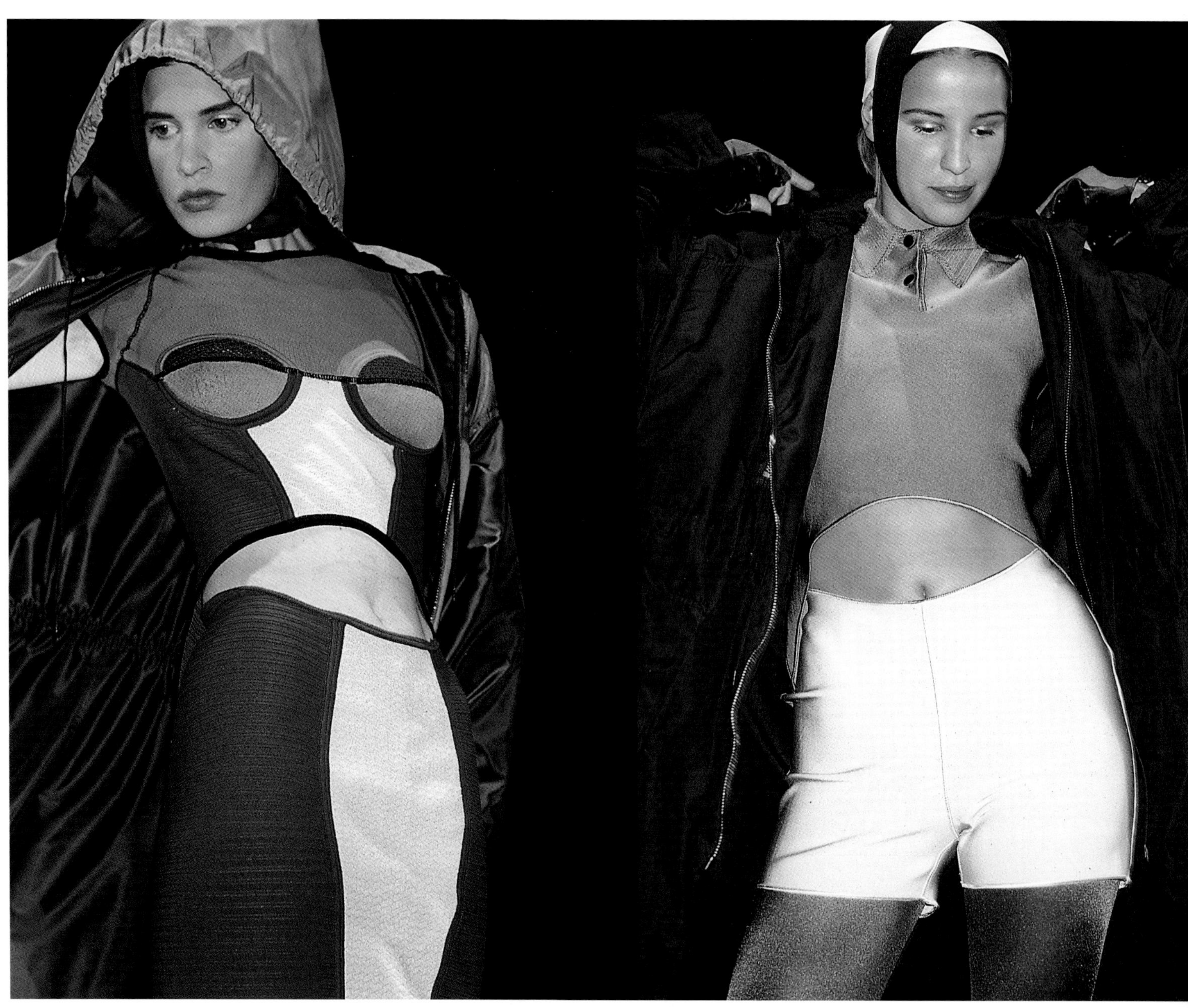

REVEALING, HIGHLIGHTING and emphasizing the female form (*left*) has been a recurring *leitmotif* in the work of Jean Paul Gaultier. He loves to outline and define the contours by his choice of fabric, cut and detailing in clothes which are a hymn to the perfection of the fit and well-toned as well as a celebration of the figure. These are examples from 'Rhapsody in Blue' Spring-Summer 1990 which combines 'classic tailoring and sportswear with a jogging feeling'.
(*Photos: Niall McInerney*)

GAULTIER HAS A WAY with stripes, whether hard or soft, horizontal or vertical, male or female. Here he uses them to great effect for clothes which would give any young man a feeling of strength and confidence. Taken from the Gaultier Jeans Collection, 'The Andro-Jeans', Spring-Summer 1993.
(*Photo: Niall McInerney*)

The idealized male torso – almost supernaturally toned and perfect – intrigues and amuses Gaultier equally. He has used models who have the real thing and has photoprinted the perfect torso on fabrics not only for men, but paradoxically, also for women. The visual pun is strong but even stronger are the questions he poses about masculine power, feminine fragility and the male-female conundrum of the importance of physical strength, bodily perfection and sexuality. The male outfit was taken from the 'Fanatics of Photography' Autumn-Winter 1992–3, while the female ensemble (*far right*) from 'Cyberbaba', Spring-Summer 1996, gave women the male hunk treatment.
(*Photos: Niall McInerney*)

'A man does not wear his masculinity in his clothes. His virility is in his head'

Like tremendous troubadors or magnificient matadors, Gaultier's men are frequently caparisoned with paillettes, bugle beads, fabulous embroidery and brilliant colour – all the things which have been denied them for the past two hundred years. Gaultier brings man back to his role as the peacock sex, although, as yet, few men have the courage to follow his lead. The above is taken from Autumn-Winter 1990–91; (*right*) from Spring-Summer 1993; (*far right*) Summer 1991. (*Photos: Niall McInerney*)

'My style has really developed through rejecting everything I learned in haute couture'

he wished to buy a flat, Jean Paul asked Lelong to lend him enough money to pay off his debts. For Lelong, the sum was not large – around £6000 – but it saved Gaultier from disgrace. Then, he had the problem of how to pay back the loan. 'I used to lie in bed' he says, 'feeling sick and thinking, I'm finished. I'm totally finished. How will I ever pay it back?'

Two things happened. Francis came in one afternoon, full of excitement, with the news that a member of the *Vogue* staff had been in the audience and he was saying that the show was very good. *Marie-Claire* and *Elle* were in agreement. Then, something even more hopeful. Dominique Emschweiller, the director of Bus Stop-Kashiyama, had been looking for a designer for some time and had been told that there was a very promising young stylist whose work she should see.

Gaultier had an interview and so impressed her that, although she had been on the verge of signing somebody else, she decided that he was the one to whom the job must go. She contacted her boss in Japan. After an agonizing weekend, Gaultier was told the news: Kashiyama would sign a contract with him for the next two years, until the end of 1981. To do so was an act of considerable faith. There were hundreds of reasons why the Japanese should not become involved with Gaultier, not least the fact, that although undoubtedly a genius, he was a wayward genius, treading

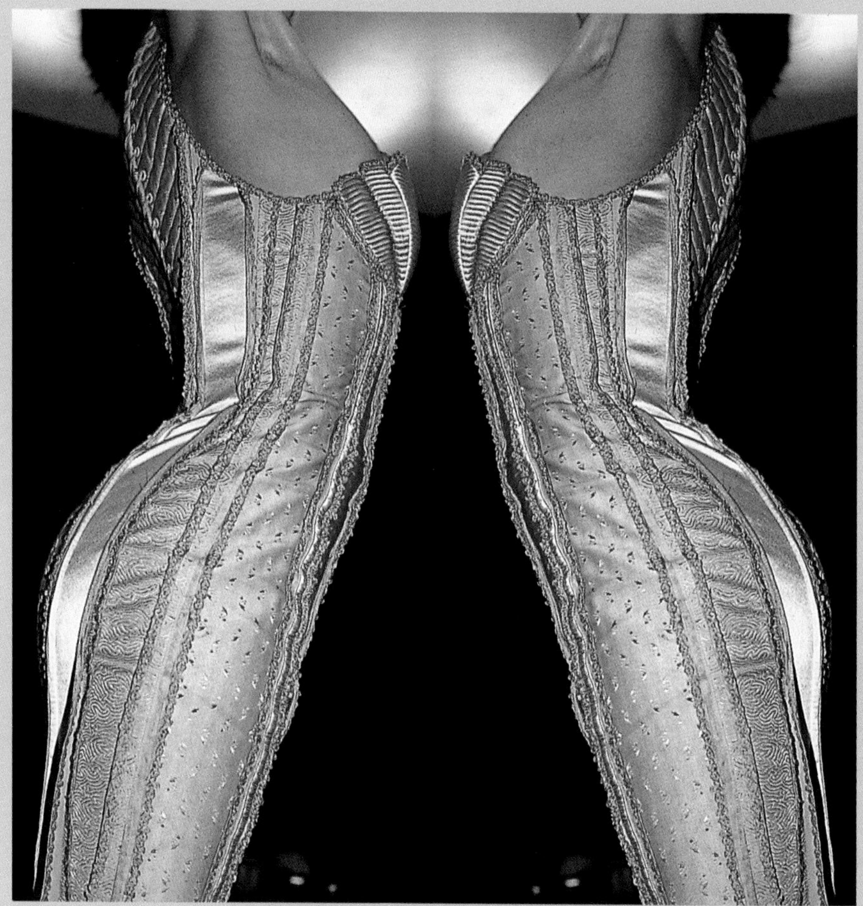

Body-consciousness is what most high fashion has been about for at least a decade and Jean Paul Gaultier is one of the foremost stormtroopers of the movement. His corset looks became part of the iconography of late twentieth-century style and he has even used complex computerized optical effects in his constant search for new ways to define our sexuality. Ensembles (*left and background right*) are from Spring-Summer 1986; while (*right*) the catsuit is taken from 'Horsewomen and Amazones of Modern Times' Autumn-Winter 1995–6. (*Photos: Niall McInerney*)

paths unfamiliar and even unknown to mainstream fashion. Clearly, he loved to elevate the banal and integrate the bizarre. He mixed the bourgeois and the outrageous. His attitude to sexuality in dress seemed to have more in common with the bordello or strip club than with the high street or drawing room. He loved things which were tacky – as he once memorably said, 'The people who dress badly, who make mistakes, are the ones who interest me' – and yet he was proud to be in the tradition of haute couture, to know not only the secret of elegance but also the perfection of the dressmaker's art at its highest level. Above all, he was a radical, questioning every preconceived idea and frequently demolishing it with a humour and confidence which belied his twenty-six years. By any standards, he presented a formidable challenge.

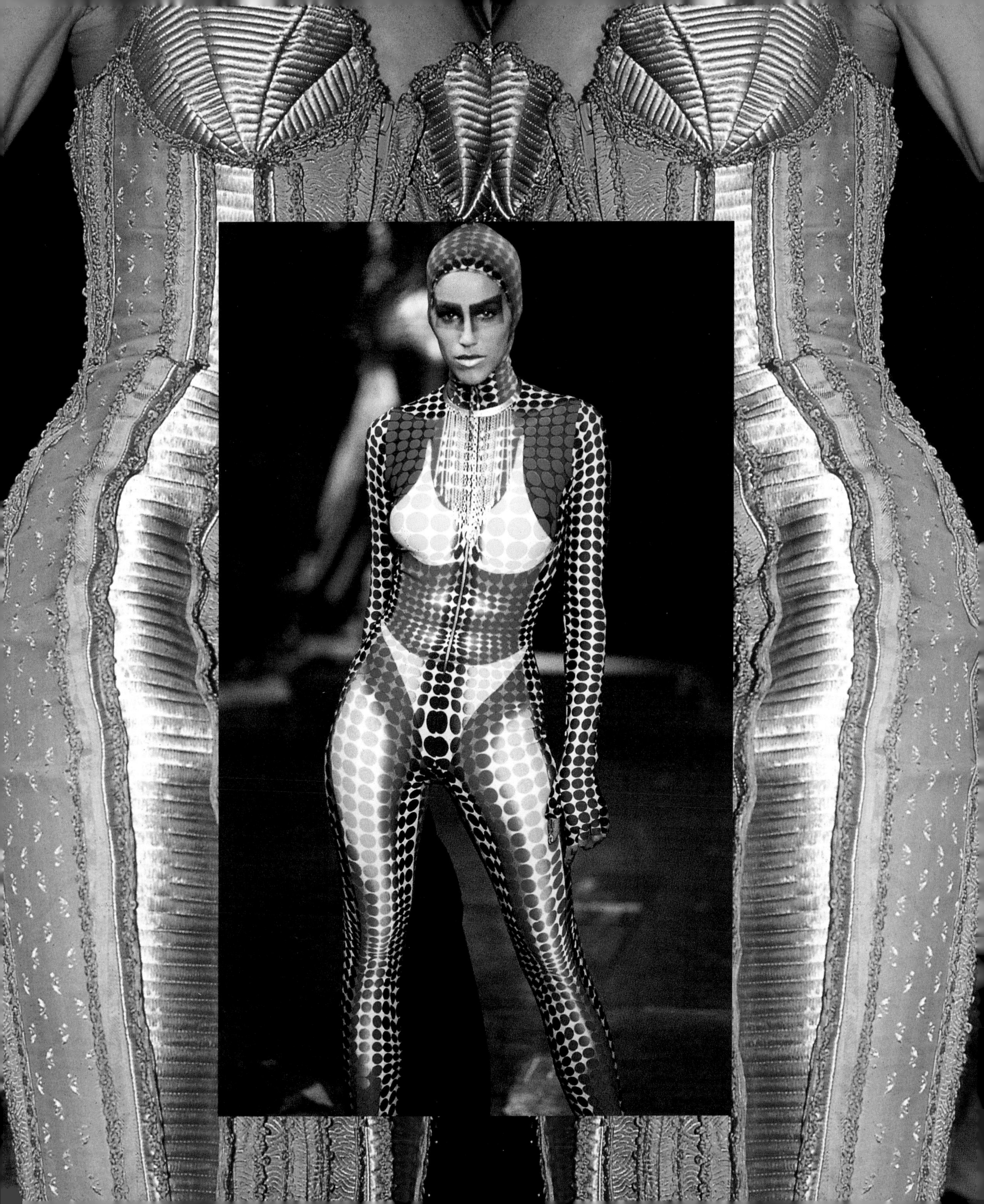

'I feel a little frightened when fashion is always to please people'

IN A PLAY on roses, thorns, crucifixion and piracy, Gaultier seems to be suggesting that there are no images which cannot be annexed by the fertile design mind. He is also having a sly dig, in his decorative exuberance, at those designers who have made themselves famous with unimaginatively sterile plain white underwear which has only a name and a logo to give it any design content, let alone distinction. From the Spring-Summer 1993 'Andro-Jean' collection. *(Photos: Niall McInerney)*

And so did his immediate task. It had taken Dominique Emschweiller some time to track down Gaultier, who had been out of Paris. And it was vital that the first collection of the new collaboration be shown in October 1978. Based on John Travolta in *Grease*, the collection included Teddy Boy hair, sleeveless T-shirts and big, bouncy skirts. By no means the greatest Gaultier collection, it satisfied the Japanese and pleased the press. It had been done at very short notice but it had been done without the spectre of financial ruin hanging over Gaultier's head. And it sold. But it was the next collection, dedicated to James Bond, which was one of Jean Paul Gaultier's favourites, although, as he admits, 'it was a catastrophe in selling'.

It soon became apparent that the Kashiyama collaboration was not going to be without friction. It was the classic fight between a designer who demanded total creative licence and the backer who needed to make commercial sense of any equation agreed between the two. Certainly, Gaultier had a fertility of imagination which was soon to make him the talking point of the world. But the Japanese didn't give up easily. When Gaultier found a new backer in the Italian industrialist firm Gibo in 1981, Kashiyama remained his licensee, and continued to give him vital backing and support.

Jean Paul Gaultier entered the eighties with confident step, although even he could not have imagined just how completely he was to make them his own. Dedicated to destroying *la règle de bon goût*, he was to succeed so thoroughly that his influence lasted well into the nineties and beyond. By his example he has influenced and encouraged young fashion designers everywhere.

page headline, declaring him as 'Paris's Court Jester' who 'entered the court of Paris titans last Friday with a wit-filled, idea-packed collection'. The *Face* was even more flattering, proclaiming him as 'the true star of Paris fashion…and his show at the faded circus arena *Cirque d'Hiver*, showed exactly why – clothes that were very wearable, very sexy and a lot of fun, sweeping riding coats…tight, tight riding jackets…red hunting coats and jodhpurs on the dishiest Algerian boys. The look was either very oversized or incredibly undersized…corsets to emphasize conical busts, ski pants worn under skirts. We raved. They craved. He'd conquered.' The same magazine, which in 1984 was exerting a world influence on the young and fashionable, described the Gaultier style as 'light, supple, humourous, uncomplicated, disconcerting but never overly bizarre. It stays close to the preoccupations of the moment without stooping to pander to them…his secret? A sort of prickly, good-natured rebellion.'

But it is Gaultier himself who best describes his 'secret' when he

Regency bucks used their dress to proclaim their masculine power. They loved the erotic frisson of stripes which curve over the body's contours, just as they adored the richness of brocades, dazzling silks and complex embroideries. Today's young dandies show the same confidence in Gaultier's modern version of items which were once standard parts of even quite modest outfits. These appeared in the 'Baroque Western' collection, Spring-Summer 1989.
(*Photos: Niall McInerney*)

and I'm glad'

J P G invited us to "compare suntans" at his packed-to-overflowing show, and he certainly gave us enough chances...as his tall, dark and undeniably handsome models showed off their bodies...But, underneath the fun-poking...were serious, sensationally cut suit jackets...*Superbe*.' The world agreed. American *Vogue*, commenting on his 1984 menswear show, saw it as 'an ode to the Third World, everything from Sinbad the Sailor to Casablanca to King Farouk in some of Paris' most originally combined clothing'. Australian *Vogue*, calling him 'wicked and witty' and praising his 'non-stop' imagination, pointed out that when you 'take away the cartoon extras...you find marvellous pieces'. *Passion*, the Paris magazine, noted that behind the sense of humour, Gaultier was a shrewd businessman. 'Printing his show invitation in *Samouri*, one of Paris' gay men's magazines and using a troupe of comics, friends and exotic muscle men as models,' it said, 'Gaultier has turned young men on to the possibilities of costume...'.

It is Gaultier's eclecticism which makes him outstanding. Unlike many of his English counterparts in the eighties – some of whom had considerable talent – he was constantly able to renew his fashion vision by cross-cultural references which covered film and pop music; the music hall he'd learned about from his grandmother; video and the popular culture of ethnic minorities. He was addicted to forties films, especially those starring Arletty, Jean Gabin, Jean Marais and Michelle Morgan. 'I was very influenced by forties elegance,' he says, 'the elegance of the gangster. The zazous. Pinstripes. Shoulders just a little too wide and very narrow at the hips. Even earlier, Cary Grant or Gary Cooper – Rudolph Valentino – they were all symbols of male sexiness. Then, later, it was Brando and James Dean, with their moodiness. They didn't just influence other men. Girls and boys were attracted to them through their sexuality, which was speaking clearly through their clothes. They were the same as Bardot and Monroe. People dreamed of them – as sex objects.' For his men's collection, 'The Male Objects', in 1984, he used as his invitation a picture of the Belgian action-movie actor Jean-Claude van Damme showing his body. 'I'm sometimes accused of being a misogynist', Gaultier says, 'But I give the men the same treatment. I make no distinction.'

Film has probably been the most powerful and consistent influence

Gaultier ended his Autumn–Winter 1998 couture collection with a bride and groom both wearing Aran cable knit, with a knitted *'Je t'aime'* across the front of his, and both sheltering under one veil. Here, as opposite, he used the rich creamy knit in his collection for Autumn-Winter 1985–6, a part of a series described by his press release as 'classic caricatures'. (*Photos: Niall McInerney*)

BECAUSE SO FEW WOMEN actually wear them today, grand evening gowns have barely changed in fifty years. Gaultier's solution is entirely contemporary. He takes traditional luxurious evening materials like taffeta, satin, chiffon and tulle and teams them with non-status relaxed materials like knitting and crochet to create a new form of modern, youthful evening wear, uniquely his own. These two examples are taken from Gaultier's Winter 1997–8 (*left*), and (*above*) from Winter 1998–9. (*Photos: Niall McInerney*)

'I have the tastes of a concierge'

on Jean Paul Gaultier. Whereas other designers talk, unconvincingly, of the effect upon them of great literature – Proust is claimed as a perennial favourite – Jean Paul admits quite openly to barely, if ever, picking up a book. When he talks of Querell of Brest, it is the Fassbinder film, not the original Genet novel, that he has in mind. He still loves the films he saw in his youth. Marcel Carné's *Les Enfants du Paradis* of 1945, starring Arletty and Jean-Louis Barrault, which he and his mother watched when it was shown on television. Carné's *L'Air de Paris* and *Drôle de Drame* are vividly remembered, as is Cocteau's 1960 classic *Le Testament d'Orphée*, starring Jean Marais.

In the eighties, Gaultier fell in love with the films of Jean-Jacques Beineix – whose 1982 film, *Diva*, became a cult classic – including *The Moon in the Gutter* and *Betty Blue*. What appeals most to the designer is Beineix's brilliance at shocking and astonishing in settings which are normal and everyday – *Diva*, his favourite, was set in contemporary Paris. Much darker is the work of another admired director, Leos Carax, who made *Boy Meets Girl* and *Bad Blood*. He has been described as having 'a cartoon-existential sensibility' – a description which could have been coined for Gaultier himself, who once briefly claimed that his favourite film was *Hairspray*, starring Divine, which projected a strip-cartoon image of fifties America as it might be seen through the eyes of a pop artist.

Pop music has been an equally important cultural influence on Gaultier. In the eighties, he was finely tuned to everything new long before it arrived in Paris – and much of it never did – because he heard it in London discos such as Heaven and immediately bought it. Sid Vicious, Boy George, Frankie Goes to Hollywood, Spandau Ballet, Sade – many of them became customers, friends and models. Marilyn, Boy George's 'gender-bender' alter-ego, appeared on Gaultier's catwalk modelling not only men's but also women's fashions. Gaultier's taste in music is as eclectic as his approach to fashion and he kept an open mind about them both in the eighties, enjoying the New Wave of Elvis Costello, Howard Devoto's band, Magazine, Blondie and Talking Heads as much as the New Romantics such as Duran Duran and Spandau Ballet or the revival of sixties' Ska by Madness, the Specials and Selecter on the Two Tone label.

It is thought by many that the spectacular show with a movie-type

'Men must learn to deal

with their fragility'

Gaultier is never happier than when he is giving us electric shocks. He mixes the unconventional with the unexpected in his constant probing of what we can accept. For many years, fashion has found nothing shocking in women wearing items of dress from the male wardrobe. Here, Gaultier is turning the tables not merely to surprise but to raise the question: *why* are we surprised? These three outfits taken from three separate collections: (*far left*) Spring-Summer 1997; (*centre left*) Autumn-Winter 1994–5; and (*above*) Winter 1996–7, prove that men's fashion can be as exotic and rewarding as women's in the hands of a confident and uninhibited designer.
(*Photos: Niall McInerney*)

title, its own *mis-en-scène* and a defile where only one outfit is worn by each model were introduced by John Galliano in the nineties. In fact, as Galliano would acknowledge, Gaultier introduced them all in the eighties – to mixed reactions.

In 1985, *Women's Wear Daily* approved a show which 'was the sort of production that could have a flourishing Off-Broadway career. It was presented as a series of vignettes that took a comic strip view of the sort of haute-bourgeois matrons who reside on Avenue Foch or Park Avenue... If it sounds like a cross between Albee and Ionesco, the clothes which these models-cum-actors were displaying with their bored, urbane saunter were unmistakably Gaultier...it was fashion spoof at its most sophisticated...he remains the number one idea man for the young market'. The *Washington Post* in the following year was less convinced. 'Gaultier always likes to be naughty and offend people with his presentations,' its report primly begins. 'But this year the man who gave the fashion world mini-sized jackets and the lace-up treatment now showing up in everyone else's spring collections, has managed to offend buyers and press...' His crime appeared to be nothing more heinous than showing 'in the old slaughterhouse section far from the centre of Paris', where 'about a hundred of Gaultier's chums and a few models waited on a stage at one end, then stepped on a rotating raised disk, then charged down a runway the length of a city block. One of the models twice thumbed her nose at the crowd...which also expressed what the designer was saying about clothes'.

Jean Paul Gaultier has often run foul of the press – in one case, quite literally. In his early eighties days, some French journalists felt that he was not just making a laughing stock of Paris couture but was also seriously endangering the city's position as a fashion leader by his clothes and shows, and the way in which he used them to debunk what he saw as some of the less realistic attitudes to high fashion found in that city. His firm belief that the old Holy Cows had to be removed if Paris was to remain in the vanguard of fashion originality didn't always receive enthusiastic support in the French press. After some particularly obtuse comments, verging, in his opinion, on the wilfully misunderstanding, Jean Paul decided to ring the changes on the traditional gifts which

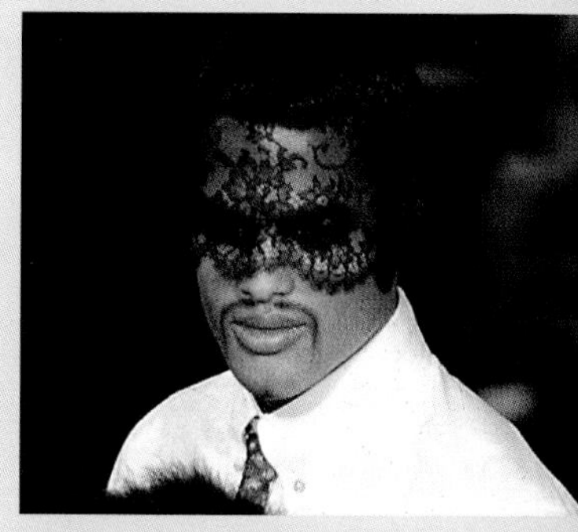

Taken from 'Couture Man', Autumn-Winter 1996–7 (*above*) a collection with a hidden agenda. Having failed to be appointed to take charge of couture at Dior, Gaultier decided to show how well he could have done the job, but in order to put the whole thing into perspective, he brought the skills and workmanshop required by couture to bear on men's, rather than women's fashion. Below, from Spring-Summer 1998.
(*Photos: Niall McInerney*)

fashion houses send to top journalists at Christmas. Instead of cavia chocolates or champagne – the boring staples – he would express the festiv spirit with the gift of turkeys. It seemed appropriate as he had received quite lot of criticism and a French expression for idiocy is 'a turkey'. Recipient included the editors of *L'Officiel*, *Depêche Mode*, *Gap* and *Elle*.

The idea was a surrealist one because the turkeys Jean Paul Gaultier sen to the press were still living. 'We thought it would be like a cartoon that come alive,' he says. 'But I suppose that it was very childish, really'. Certainly, i proved a nightmare for everyone at Gaultier, as well as the recipients. Keepin them in the studio for a week before they were sent off in huge boxes to th selected journalists traumatized the whole staff. 'Imagine!', he laughs. 'Twelv turkeys! All smelling bad!'

Another time in the eighties, Gaultier quarrelled with a journalist abou the principle of fairness and lack of prejudice – both causes for which he wi accept no compromise. 'It was for a menswear show in which most of th models were black. A particular French journalist, using the slogan for washing powder, wrote *Omo Le Plus Blanc*. I thought it was insulting to me outrageously insulting to many models and a classic example of petit-bourgeoi French anti-homosexual fascism.' he says. 'I could not rest until I had take revenge. I sent her twenty-five packets of Omo.' He also claims to have give her telephone number to a lesbian and gay introduction switchboar suggesting that she was looking for a 'dominant mistress'.

Despite this, Jean Paul Gaultier claims that he accepts criticism – provide it is just, informed and without prejudice. 'It is the risk you take if you show he says. 'And, to do so is, in a way, pretentious, so you must be prepared t admit that people may have views which do not coincide with yours. As lon as the critics know what they were talking about, I have no difficulty if the don't like what I do. But fashion commentary is very political and, in som cases, I suspect the criticism has a hidden agenda, with nothing to do with th clothes. If one talent rises, another sinks. I know that. I expect it. But I don always accept it. Advertisements are the clue to how you are received. If it is poor show – and we all have those, now and again – advertising revenue ca save you. The comments in the magazine are written ambiguously. There room for a kind or unkind interpretation of the words. But, withou advertising, you can be destroyed – and the people who do it are perfectl

THE OLD CLICHE of the male as *victor ludorum*, champion of the world, has never fooled Gaultier. Here he takes the trappings of athletic prowess – the victor's belt, the gladiatorial glove and the ruthless leather of gangsters or secret police – and overemphasizes them so that they no longer seem real, almost as if he felt the same way about the men who dress this way. (*Photos: Niall McInerney*)

'Humour must be a natural part of clothing'

'There are far too many clothes, boutiques and fashion designers'

successful commercial designers working in Europe. It was backed up by brilliant advertising campaigns on which he worked with Jean-Baptiste Mondino, considered by many to be *the* great original force in French photography in the eighties. Witty and provocative, they were seminal images on the level of Jean Paul Goude's projections of Grace Jones, and they reflected Mondino's video-making background. In fact, he and Gaultier made a video in 1988, the year the designer introduced his cheaper collection, Junior Gaultier, for a single released by Gaultier called *House Couture, Aow Tou Dou Zat*, or *How to Do That.* A mixture of snatches of a Selina Scott interview for the British television programme, *The Clothes Show*, Edith Piaf, jazz and the sounds of animals in a barn, it has Gaultier's voice linking everything together. The video was shot in a huge studio outside Paris and was, Gaultier admits, a piece of self-indulgence for him and Mondino. As he said at the time, 'We're only doing it for fun. It's an image record. I don't want to be a pop star...and I certainly don't think I can sing...The video wasn't designed to sell either the record or my clothes, so we were both completely free. There were no barriers.'

Pop videos and remixed singles seem an entirely appropriate obsession for the man who admits to watching mainly MTV and VH-1, but many thought that, even for somebody rapidly becoming Europe's pop culture polymath, his decision to become involved in ballet was a wayward one. In fact, he became interested in the idea because he could see that, like French fashion, the dance in France required revitalizing. A great admirer of the dancer and choreographer Regine Chopinet, he collaborated with her on a piece called *Le Defile*, which was a danced fashion show based on costumes he designed especially for the performance. It created sufficient interest in France for it to be also performed in New York. *Le Defile*, it hardly needs saying, was not in the tradition of classical ballet. Chopinet used videos, back projections and even non-dancers brought up on stage from the audience – all set to

JAPONISME swept Paris in the late nineteenth century – fans, dragons and feathers were everywhere. Gaultier updates them all – but with his own unique slant – either garnishing a pink satin evening gown with fans, allowing rampant dragons embroidered in silk to race across a skirt with heavy silk fringing and tassels, or festooning a feather-printed fabric with even more feathers in order to match the richness and opulence of the other two designs. From his Spring-Summer couture collections of 1988 (*centre*) and 1999 (*left and right*).
(*Photo: Niall McInerney*)

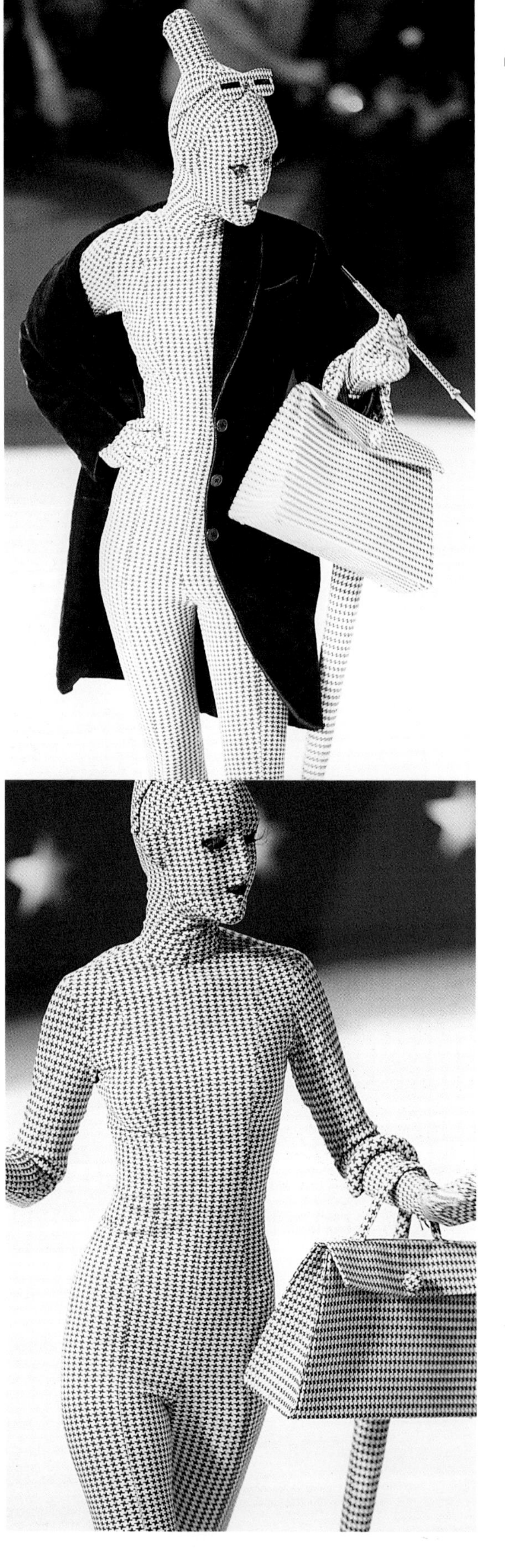

'It's always the badly-dressed people who are the most interesting'

specially created music. As Gaultier explains, 'She is not limited to seeing dance only as dancing, she creates different expressions by her multi-media approach. The first time I saw something by Chopinet I realized that we shared a common language. She made dance fun – and funny – almost like a cartoon. It was a language I could understand.'

It was all part of a growing involvement in the arts at all levels, including television spectaculars. As early as 1985, Gaultier had worked on a New Year's Day documentary programme on Shiela, one of his pop star heroines, in which, as the press hand-out said, he helped to reveal the hitherto unknown faces of the singer by exploring new possibilities for her image. The show was sponsored by Jack Lang's Ministry of Culture.

The decade was to end for Jean Paul Gaultier on a high note. He had become a world figure, famous in a way unique to himself. He was unlike any other designer on earth, not just because of his fashion approach but also for his honesty. It is impossible to imagine any of his fellow established couturiers in Paris or Milan admitting, as he did, as early as 1985, to the *Face*, that, in over twenty shows at that point, he only thought five were hot favourites and the rest 'have been mediocre, and one or two, embarrassingly bad'. But that did not stop him making money, including that from a design deal with the European wedding dress specialists Pronuptia, as well as his many own lines.

At least one element in the many areas in which Jean Paul Gaultier would become involved in the nineties was presaged in 1989 when he designed costumes for Peter Greenaway's *The Cook, The Thief, His Wife and Her Lover*, dressing Helen Mirren in provocatively sexy fashion. Film was to interest him increasingly in the coming decade.

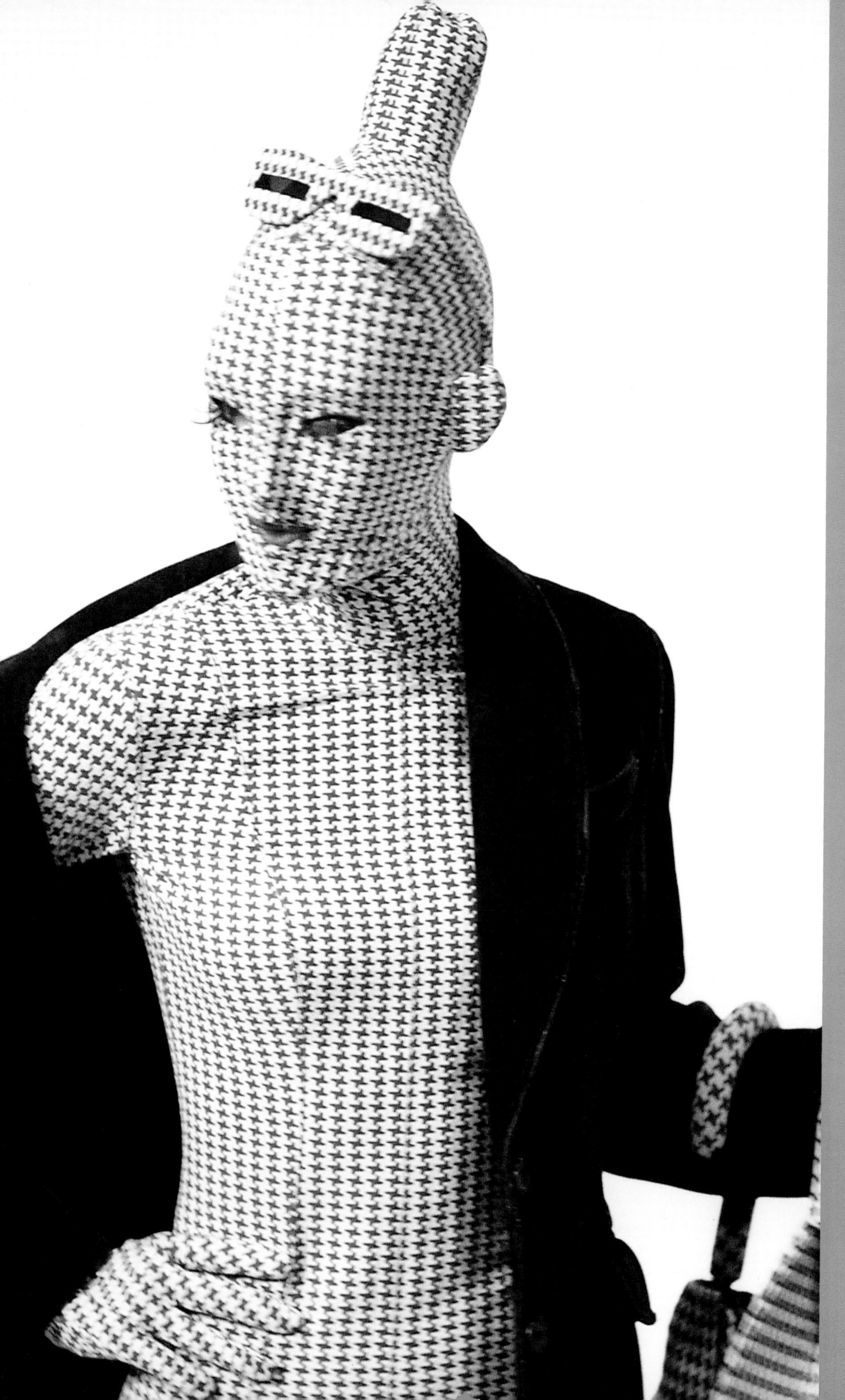

Too great an addiction to fashion can easily end up at a point where the personality of the wearer disappears under the fashion statement. It is this sinister side of dress to which Gaultier is drawing attention with this unnerving model whose face has been entirely eclipsed by the chic anonymity of the powerfully graphic material. Her appearance in Gaultier's womenswear collection 'French Can-Can' Autumn-Winter 1991–2, had a electrifying effect on the audience and loses none of its sinister power in the photographic image. (*Photos: Niall McInerney*)

'What m
people w
who

5 POLISHING UP THE POLYMATH

JEAN PAUL GAULTIER BEGAN the new decade in a typically jokey way, publishing his life story in a book called *A Nous Deux la Mode*, which was a photographic strip cartoon featuring actors portraying key moments in his life, interspersed with real-life 'guest' appearances by the couturier, his managing director Donald Potard and current friends. Inspired in its tacky references to the cheap photo-romances which are a staple of the French literary underbelly, its cover is a photograph of Gaultier as an air-brushed *ingenue* clutching a bouquet of daisies and surrounded by more, and with a phallic Eiffel Tower penetrating a deep blue sky. It is a kitsch masterpiece by his favourite photographers, Pierre et Gilles, whose carefully contrived portraits – usually of young men – are prized in the gay world as camp classics. Francis Menuge died of Aids in 1990, so the book can be seen as a memorial to the role he had played in building the house of Gaultier into one of the most successful fashion enterprises of the eighties. The effect of his death took Gaultier a long time to overcome.

It was helped by the excitement of a commission from Madonna. Lionel Vermeil tells how it happened: 'Jean Paul rarely has a rehearsal for a show, but this time he decided that he would. This meant that I had to remain late in the office until the models were released from other shows so that I could collect them and take them to the rehearsal. The phone rang and I picked it up, expecting news about the models still outstanding. A voice said, "Hi! I'm Herb Ritts. Madonna is working on her next tour and wants to know if Monsieur Gaultier will do the costumes?" I was very surprised, but also delighted. I knew how much Jean Paul admired Madonna but I decided that the night before a show was *not* the time to discuss it, so I kept it to myself. After the show, I told him and *he* was also delighted.'

Dressing the *Blonde Ambition* world tour of 1990, videoed as *Like a Virgin*, was a commission straight from heaven for Gaultier. No designer and client could be more in tune than he and Madonna – in their attitudes to fashion, sex, performance and outrage. The designer who had once said, 'I have always been afraid of anything too abstract' knew that the performer would want him to produce designs which would be as direct and specific as her act. It was agreed almost without saying that the central theme would be the corset look which had attracted Madonna to

JUST AS HE PUT men in skirts so Gaultier was one of the pioneers of underwear being worn as outerwear. It is a play which he has enjoyed since the eighties, developing endless variation on the themes of the boned and stiffened bra and the corset – both obsessions which have been with him since childhood. These two examples from his Spring-Summer 1987 collection are the image of what is conjured by the words, Jean Paul Gaultier, in the average, non-fashion person's mind, so powerfully has he made this particular statement about fashion, femininity and a possible route to future glamour.
(Photos: Niall McInerney)

Gaultier in the first place, but there were other costumes to be decided on also, such as the filmy peignoir look and the femme fatale.

Jean Paul's imagination went back to the costumes he'd designed for Annie Girardot, the star at the Casino de Paris, in 1982, the same year in which he told a French journalist that his ideal woman – *'la plus fatale du cinema Hollywoodien'* was Bette Davis. Interestingly, one of the stage goddesses with whom Madonna was to be compared in looks was the young Bette Davis, and rather as the earlier Hollywood star behaved with her costume designers, Madonna was incisive, making her decision on the sketches instantly. She knew precisely what she wanted – and so did Gaultier.

'My shows have always been sexual because sex and sexuality are everywhere'

It was a commission that raised the Gaultier profile even higher than it had been in the eighties. Then, his name had become important enough in Europe and in Britain – he was even featured in the British satirical political television programme *Spitting Image* – but now he was 'big time' in Los Angeles, within the music business as well as film. It seemed the whole world knew him. His European – and specifically British – profile was also raised by his role as co-presenter with Antoine de Caunes in the late-night Channel 4 programme, *Eurotrash*. A huge popular hit, with peak viewing figures of over two million, it is, interestingly, the one Gaultier enterprise not mentioned in the designer's official biography handed out to journalists. Is it omitted because the house of Gaultier regrets Jean Paul's involvement or is it ignored as not being germaine to his work as a designer?

Eurotrash was brilliantly named. Its title precisely summed up its content. In a direct line stretching from *The Goon Show* and *Monty Python's Flying Circus* – although neither as clever nor as witty – its brief was to expose the ludicrous side of human behaviour, in two particular areas: the sexual and the lavatorial. Gaultier jumped at the opportunity to break through middle-class hypocritical attitudes and middle-aged preconceptions of what was 'suitable' for airing in public and what was

With Gaultier, wit and outrage are never far below the surface, ready to bubble up with the exuberance which has always made his shows such great entertainment. No-one knows better when to send out a showstopper such as this *trompe l'oeil* body reminiscent of Josephine Baker – with the added outrage of a touch of irresistable 'caviar' into the bargain. From his Spring-Summer 1993 collection. *(Photo: Niall McInerney)*

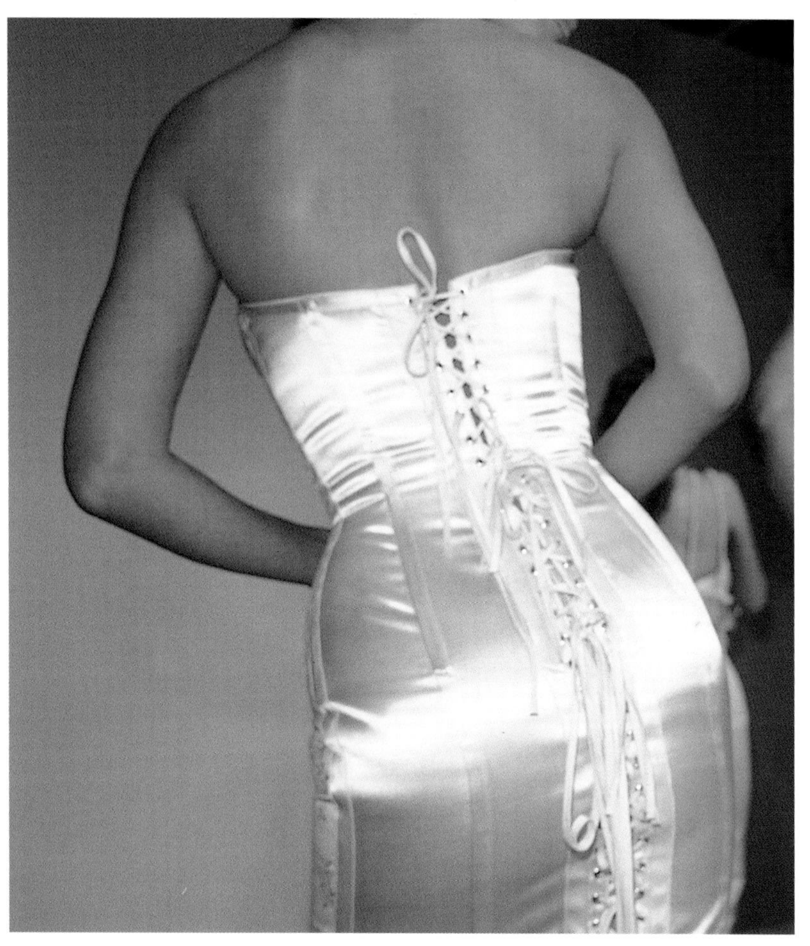

CORSET LACING AND shiny satin have been Gaultier's trademarks since 1983, when this Marilyn Monroe-type derriere first hit his catwalk in a collection called 'Dadaism', which featured underwear dresses and the first Gaultier corsets in a series of garments based on body movements. It was a theme which he was to rework many times in the coming years. In one form or another, it's hardly missed a season since.
(*Photos: Niall McInerney*)

not. It was part of the battle against mealy-mouthed conformity which he had been fighting through his fashion attitudes for well over a decade. For him, it was more than just an opportunity to make *double-entendre* remarks, dress up in various costumes and have fun with TV footage of beer served in chamberpots, penis-shaped bread and rat stroganoff. It was not just about laddish excitement over the bared breasts of La Cicciolina, the Italian porn star turned politician, or the ludicrously unlikely instructions for having sex in a tree. It was about subverting the sterile canons of taste which divide generations. When the *The Times* wrote in disbelief that it had never suspected European culture could stoop so low, it made the point by missing the point. *Eurotrash* and its phenomenal viewing figures made clear that European culture had changed.

The programme was almost universally condemned. *Private Eye* called it 'the most tawdry, nipple-heavy, genitally-fixated, excrement-encrusted entertainment series yet seen on British television'. *Time Out* took a slightly more sophisticated approach, claiming it to be a show that 'pulls together the camp, the kitsch and the eye-poppingly weird', adding that Gaultier was a 'natural in front of the camera' – a view endorsed by the series editor, Peter Stuart, who said of his performance, 'Jean Paul has adapted incredibly to the television medium...He'll sometimes play the bimbo but, of course, he's a very bright man.' In what might be seen as a damage-limitation comment, Gaultier pointed out, 'although I love all the eccentricity, I am very conservative too.'

Although the programme was so popular, many commentators believe that it affected Gaultier's status as a designer and was responsible for the slump in his influence, which was seen by some as a feature of the first half of the decade for the house of Gaultier. Others believe *Eurotrash* had nothing to do with it, claiming that, after such a phenomenally

ALTHOUGH THE pointed bra was first taken from Africa and shown on a European catwalk by Yves Saint Laurent in 1967, Gaultier's re-invention of it in the mid-eighties really put it on the fashion map. Although in its extreme form (*far right*) it has no life away from the catwalk, the conical bra not only redefines breasts as two erogenous zones – what else led to all those breast implants and injections of the past ten years – it created an approach whereby underwear details became fashion – and that led to the slip dress and much more besides, which we take for granted today. An example of underwear adapted to outerwear (*right*) in Gaultier's trail-blazing show of Summer 1983, the first bat-squeak of what was to come. By Autumn-Winter 1984–5 (*far right*) it had grown into a clarion cry to throw off inhibitions and join in the fun. It made Gaultier's particular fashion approach a talking point far beyond the confines of the fashion world because it was not just an attitude to dress but a questioning of how to treat female sexuality.
(*Photos: Niall McInerney*)

GAULTIER HAS BEEN criticized for indulging homosexual fantasies in much of his menswear but it is important to remember that he explores the fetishist dream of raunchy female sexuality in the same unconditional way. These pages reveal the things which have interested him over the years, from cage dresses, like the hooped skirts of Victorian crinolines, to the chains and constraints of the S & M world, the allure of semi-nakedness and, inevitably, the corset dress, all of which have exerted considerable influence not only on dress but on how people saw femininity in the late twentieth century. Taken from various collections: (*above left*) Autumn-Winter 1990–91; (*above right and right*) Spring-Summer 1989; (*facing page, left*) Spring-Summer 1995, dedicated to the end of the century; (*facing page, right*) Autumn-Winter 1983–4, an early example of a combination used many times by Gaultier. (*Photos: Niall McInerney*)

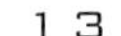

ONCE THE imagination is released there are no constraints on a designer's possibilities. Here, for Winter 1987, Gaultier explores the world of Barbarella using rubber, plastic and traditional materials in a glorious space-age mixture which even today is arresting in its originality. These examples are from his collection 'Forbidden Gaultier' for Autumn-Winter 1987–8, which brought together an alliance of the traditional and technological. (*Photos: Niall McInerney*)

successful period in the eighties, an eclipse was inevitable in a world as volatile and novelty-fixated as fashion. Fashion journalists – some of whom have an unrealistic concept of the dignity of their calling – found it hard to take seriously the fashion of a man they felt was becoming a media clown prince. Gaultier rejects suggestions that he was spending too much time on the television series and not enough on his collections, claiming that it took only a few evenings per month to record his contribution. His reason for leaving the show after five very successful series was that, the range of interest being so narrow, it was becoming repetitive because it was impossible to find new subjects. Those close to him feel that he merely became bored.

With the show, maybe, but certainly not with life. In 1992, he launched his 'Gaultier Jeans' collection and also presented a retrospective

'My clothes are very exhibitionist'

of his collections in Los Angeles for Amfar, the Aids research charity. It was a spectacular evening, with many of the clothes modelled by top actresses. Madonna wore a breast-revealing pinstriped pinafore dress; Raquel Welch wore a fitted body with gloves in Gaultier's 'cage' strips and Faye Dunaway wore his cut-away riding coat and thigh-high feathered boots. It was a packed social occasion, proving that the 'bustier man', as he was sometimes called, had lost none of his crowd-pulling power.

In April 1993, Gaultier launched his first perfume. Compared with other designers, he had left it very late in his career. But what he had lost in time, he made up for in impact. If there was any real problem with profits and turnover for his business in the early nineties, the launch of the Gaultier women's fragrance was to turn things around dramatically. At its US unveiling in Saks Fifth Avenue, New York, it broke the store's record for a perfume launch, taking $300,000 in retail sales in its first full week. Like everything else Gaultier does, it was carefully balanced to intrigue and shock in equal degrees – both in its packaging and its scent. But it was also delicately poised so that the wit and outrage outweighed everything else. It was, as he said, a scent which echoed not only his fashion approach but also his attitudes to life.

It was presented in a tin can of the kind which had inspired Gaultier to create a range of jewellery years before. He explained his choice by pointing out that a can was part of American culture and, by using it, he had aimed at a balance between the outside, 'a symbol of industry and repetition', and the inside, 'which is very feminine'. As he explained, 'The contradiction makes a harmony'. Certainly, it was a typical Gaultier conceit to put something very luxurious, like perfume, normally to be treasured, in something very cheap, like a can, usually to be thrown away. Backed by Shiseido and created by Beauté Prestige International, its appearance was like nothing seen before, and old hands in the business of perfume launches were openly declaring that if it succeeded they would

walk away from their jobs because it would mean that anything goes.

And it did succeed. Not only was the tin can intriguing to people, the bottle itself was unexpected and yet totally in keeping with how the public generally conceived Gaultier's spirit. It was in the shape of a woman in a corset. Inevitably, it carried echoes of Schiaparelli's late thirties perfume, 'Shocking', the bottle for which was reputedly based on the mannequin used to make clothes for Mae West. Whether it was a question of two wayward geniuses of one mind or whether Gaultier had been influenced by 'Shocking' is irrelevant. By putting his signature corset over the bottle, he made his idea not only original but also entirely modern. As was the fragrance itself, described by Gaultier in the *New York Times* as having a note of nail polish remover, 'like you're smelling the gas in sparkling water', 'a touch of vanilla to make you salivate', and a faint whiff of 'the powder of my grandmother when I was a child, that smell of oldish powder'.

Gaultier's popularity reasserted itself in the fashion and fragrance worlds, although it had not dropped at all with the young who followed his fashions and his doings almost as avidly as they followed everything to do with their pop idols. But there was a slight blip. Jean Paul Gaultier's women's collection for 1993–4 had been an *hommage* to the dress of Hassidic Jews. Called 'The Chic Rabbis', it featured long narrow coats, a silhouette with virtually no body emphasis, and elegant, wide fur hats. The show had received muted praise, not for political reasons but because, to many, used to Gaultier's outrageous sexual fireworks, it was a little disappointing. It was photographed, elegantly, in a Jewish quarter of Brooklyn, by a German photographer, Ellen von Unswerth.

When the pictures appeared in French *Vogue* they caused a rumpus in Paris, but the house of Gaultier maintains that those who thought it insensitive to base a collection on a persecuted minority was small. They insist that they received very many more calls and letters praising them than criticizing. It was, perhaps, a storm in a teacup but, for a man who always maintains that clothes are part of life, a reflection of attitudes and therefore political, Gaultier's reaction was not especially relaxed. 'Nowadays', he says, 'you feel that whatever you want to create, you need to consult a lawyer first.' His explanation now, well after the event, is that

'London and Paris are my world'

GAULTIER HERE USES corsets for their original purpose, to emphasize breasts and buttocks in an exuberent eighteenth-century mixture reminiscent of Moll Flanders and the many heroines rolled in the hay in the picaresque novels of Fielding, Richardson and Smollett.
(*Photos: Niall McInerney*)

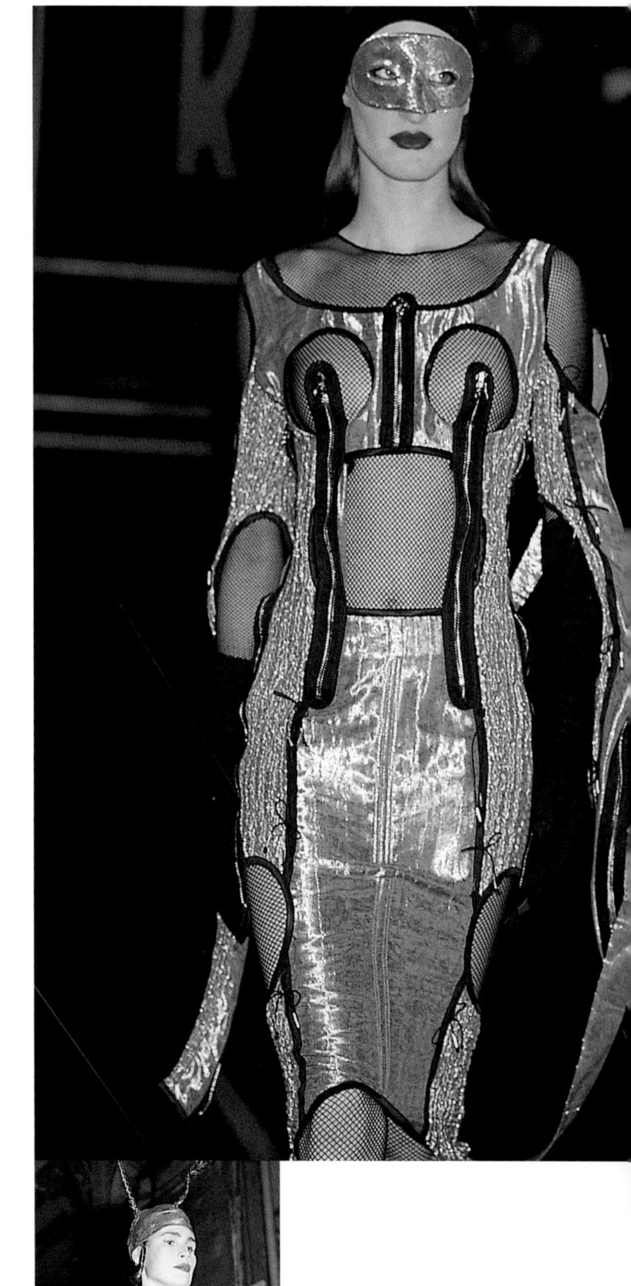

there was nothing ambiguous about the Jewish collection, 'Although,' he adds, 'it was, perhaps, a little pretentious. I think Jewish dress is beautiful and it reflects a strong culture. After all, I'm a Catholic, but that still doesn't prevent me from using crosses in fashion.'

Working with another Catholic, the cult Spanish film-maker, Pedro Almodóvar, on his tenth feature film, *Kika*, gave Gaultier the opportunity to further ruffle the feathers of complacency. His costume designs for Victoria Abril as Andrea Caracortada, the evil force pursuing the heroine, were an outrageous mixture of high camp, sci-fi and fetishist fantasies of the dominatrix rampant. Helmets sporting cameras, searchlights instead of breasts and rubber dresses slashed and dripping with blood were all part of the wardrobe. As he explained, 'Almodóvar wanted a mixture of glamour, pop and punk. Victoria's clothes were deliberately aggressive, like her black leather overalls with scarlet clasps...It was fascinating to do but I don't think that is the future of fashion.' The film was released early in 1994 and was not considered one of Almodóvar's best.

In November 1994 the *Financial Times* published a list which it had compiled by consulting an international cross-section of buyers, editors and industry specialists to find out where the true fashion influence lay. In the section 'Most Creative Designer', Gaultier was way ahead with 26.9 per cent of the votes. He was second in the 'Most Copied Designer' category and joint fourth in the 'Most Covetable Collection' group. Eighteen months later, in a similar straw-poll conducted by *Le Journal des Textiles* by canvassing international publications such as French *Vogue*, *Die Welt*, *La Stampa* and the *New York Times*, he beat Galliano to first place by 56 points, although six months after that he had slipped to fourth place, despite the fact that, in September 1994, he had replaced his Junior Gaultier label with a new and cheaper line called JPG.

It was also in 1994 that Gaultier designed his third film, this time taking responsibility for all of the costumes. *La Cité des Enfants Perdus* by Pierre Jeunet and Marc Caro was based on the German fable *The Pied Piper of Hamlyn*, brought up to date with a mad scientist and evil Siamese twins called the Octopus, for whom he made severe Lotte Lenya-type tailored suits joined at the hip, reminiscent of the double mackintosh for lovers which he created in the late seventies while at Cardin – but, this time, his

When the Spanish film-maker Pedro Almodóvar invited Gaultier to create costumes for the star Victoria Abril (*bottom right*), in *Kika*, filmed in 1994, the couturier re-created the late-eighties mood of his domatrice collections. As with them, so for the film, he had great fun playing with our sexual fantasies. In both cases, it was all gloriously tongue in cheek and outrageously high camp – in short, Jean Paul Gaultier at his extravagant best.
(*Photo from Kika: Jean Marie Leroy*)

From the 'Forbidden Gaultier' collection Autumn-Winter 1987–8 (*facing page, below*); outfits taken from 'Women Among Women' Autumn-Winter 1989–90 (*facing page above, this page above left and centre*); and an early example of outrage from Spring-Summer 1985 (*above*).
(*Photos: Niall McInerney*)

job was to give the garment fascist overtones. Caro, art director of the film, praised Gaultier for being 'able to integrate his personal vision within the universe of the film', adding, 'We both believe in the extremes of beauty, which many people find bizarre.' Gaultier claimed that he was working in the old tradition of French film, where the visual approach was vitally important. He told the *New York Times* that the film was 'a mixture of all the things I truly love, a mixture of Jack-the-Ripper London, the Eiffel Tower and Captain Nemo. There was a strong connection. In my boutique, my shop and my buildings in Paris there are many things like that.' Gaultier's film, Luc Besson's sci-fi thriller, *The Fifth Element*, starring Bruce Willis, was set in the twenty-third century. Besson told *Entertainment*: 'I wanted the best and that is Jean Paul. He knows the colour and flavour of New York.' Gaultier's comments were more down to earth. He called the futuristic costumes he designed for the flight attendants, 'a little change from what they are wearing on Air France'.

Things were happening behind the scenes in Paris fashion in the mid-nineties which were to have a considerable impact on Gaultier. Bernard Arnault, head of the Möet Chandon-Louis Vuitton luxury conglomerate, had begun to look for a designer to replace Gianfranco Ferré at Dior ready for the fiftieth anniversary of the house's foundation in 1947. Gaultier claims that he was approached to discuss the job two years before John Galliano was appointed to be creative director of Christian Dior. He sketched out some ideas for Monsieur Arnault to see – and waited. He had been told that the firm would require whoever they appointed to produce ready-to-wear and couture collections – a considerable load on top of his own Gaultier collection. But he was prepared to do it because the idea of couture attracted him very much. Even ten years earlier, when Christian Lacroix had left Patou in order to set up his own fashion house – also, as it happens, an Arnault-funded enterprise – Gaultier had made a forward-looking and original suggestion to the firm where he had earlier worked.

'At that time', he says, 'There were several of us who wanted to do couture – Montana, Mugler, Alaïa and me in Paris, Vivienne Westwood in London and Romeo Gigli in Milan. In fact, most of us were already working almost to couture levels. I suggested to the house of Patou that

NOT ALL Gaultier's sexual references are to do with the domatrice. He has a gentler, more lyrical approach which is perhaps more typical of the real man. Gossamer-fine robes are as commonly seen on his runways as the remarkably innocent undress

which seems to come from eighteenth-century novels. An outstanding example of couture workmanship (*facing page left*) from 1998 and his corset dress from Spring-Summer 1992. (*Photos: Niall McInerney; drawing: Gladys Perint Palmer*)

PANNIERS, A STAPLE of eighteenth-century fashionable dress, evolved from the sixteenth-century bum roll. Both were created to add volume and therefore importance to the female form, but also to create the illusion of a narrow waist and suggest good child-bearing potential. Gaultier re-created them for the late nineties not only in their traditional form but also as an architectural feature for a suit where the masculine collar and tie are in pointed contrast to the femininity of the hip interest. Both examples are from Gaultier's couture collection for Summer 1998. (*Photos: Niall McInerney*)

we all take it in turns to make a couture collection for them. It would have been perfectly possible because Patou really had no house style. It didn't have the strong personality of Dior or Saint Laurent. So, each designer could have done a collection per season. Patou's immediate response? "Too expensive". They didn't even consider it. That is *so* French. We weren't even asking for money!'

He is honest about the Dior situation. 'Six months before they appointed John, I was secretly informed that Monsieur Arnault disliked my association with *Eurotrash*. He felt it was inconsistent with the importance of the role at Dior. I was also secretly told that he felt it would be an embarrassment if, as design director at Dior, I ever had to meet the Princess of Wales – although *I* have been secretly told that she often watched *Eurotrash*. But, at the end of the day, *I* didn't refuse. Dior refused.'

But he did refuse Arnault's offer of Givenchy – a post eventually to go to another English designer, Alexander McQueen. 'Mainly', Gaultier says, 'because I never admired the work of Givenchy. He never had any style, in my view, and it was always an "old" house. He never made me dream in the way I dreamt of being an assistant to Yves Saint Laurent when I was young. And to arrive after John? No. I told Arnault that I prefer to open my own couture house. He replied, "That, I don't recommend. Don't do it. It costs".' But Gaultier did. Although he admits that it makes him lose a lot of money, he adds, 'it's my little luxury'.

It would not be like Jean Paul Gaultier to make a conventional entry into couture. He determined that, in a climate where Dior and Givenchy were endlessly discussed, he would find his own way. And he did. Jean Paul Gaultier presented his first couture collection for Autumn–Winter 1996–7, in January 1996, four months after he had launched 'Le Male', his fragrance for men, packaged in the same way as his women's perfume had been and backed by an advertising campaign by Mondino, featuring a twenty-three year old Cuban model, David Fumero, dressed as a sailor and arm-wrestling with himself.

'The Couture Man' was a pastiche. Based on his often-expressed belief that men should be allowed equality with women, he presented his clothes exactly as couture used to be presented in the fifties. There was no music, and a man dressed in black, like an old-style directrice, stood on the stairs and announced each entry: 'Outfit Number One. *Tailleur Trotteur*.' Not only was each outfit named in the classic couture manner but also the rhythm of the show followed the old style: daywear, cocktail and evening wear, ending with the grand soiré. Finally, the 'bride', wearing an outfit called *Le Plus Belle Jour*. The show caused a sensation for its wit, irrelevance and style. Many claimed – not entirely correctly – that only Gaultier had the knowledge of couture to sustain such a spoof. Certainly, everything shown was made to the highest levels of couture, but it was to be another year before Jean Paul launched *Gaultier Paris*, his couture collection for women and his answer to Bernard Arnault.

Lionel Vermeil recalls the show as a very emotional occasion, because 'it was the beginning of something; a fresh start. People who had loved and supported his work were afraid he was going to change. And people who had discounted him because he didn't do couture began to reassess him. But it changed the rhythm of the house. Before couture, Jean Paul had been a sprinter: he would make a great deal of effort and work hard, and then he could rest. But when he added couture to his other collections, he became marathon man, always running. By doing it himself, without Dior or Givenchy as backers, Jean Paul is both more and less free. More, because he answers to himself alone. Less, because he has to think of the money all the time.'

In 1997, Gaultier had another of his political disagreements. And it made him pleased he had preserved his independence. He had decided that his Autumn-Winter 1997–8 collection would be dedicated to black culture as a tribute to Nina Simone and Miriam Makeba. It would be entirely shown on black models. At the same time, the French government passed a law to limit immigration, so what had begun as an aesthetic decision by Gaultier had, by the time of the show, become a political one – as so much of his work in the last twenty years has been. As he says, 'Being homosexual, I think about minorities a lot. There are times when you must take a position. Individuals always feel vulnerable and want to hide. But that is never the way. You can't be frightened and run away. Our everyday life is the fruit of politics and the only way to make it work is by getting together and fighting.'

People don't come from Jean Paul Gaultier's background and enter

THE POWER OF post-revolutionary Soviet graphics, and the experiments by artists like Rodchenko in the twenties to find a form of non-status dress for the proletariat have exerted considerable influence on twentieth-century thinking about design, but surprisingly had little effect on fashion until Gaultier's 'Constructivist' Russian collection for Autumn-Winter 1986–7, which captured all the power of the original and was taken up by the designers of motorbike leathers who are still following his guidelines today. Gaultier himself considers this one of his most important and influential collections and it was also memorable for its presentation. Each of the 120 models wore one outfit only and all were on stage at the same time. Gaultier was also one of the models. (*Photos: Niall McInerney*)

ПОЛ
ПУБЛИ

THE DECORATIVE possibilities of the dress code of the Hassidic Jewish sect – from their magnificent fur hats to their strictly tailored long coats – excited Gaultier, who realized that here was elegance and confidence which could be used for high fashion. His 'Chic Rabbis' collection of Autumn-Winter 1993–4 was sensationally strong, although it was to bring political repercussions. Gaultier genuinely presented it as an homage to Jewish people but it caused offence in many quarters. The subsequent fuss has clouded the real signficance of the collection, which marked a move away from past obsessions.
(*Photos: Niall McInerney; drawing: Gladys Perint Palmer*)

a highly specialized world in which, having no practical training, they have to rely on enthusiasm, determination and belief in self, without learning how to fight. Confidence and dedication are developed by the individual constantly measuring himself against other practitioners of his craft. We discover much about Jean Paul Gaultier by learning what he thinks of his peers. One of the last – along with Christian Lacroix – to be trained in the old methods, his judgement of couturiers is more valuable than the opinions of younger designers because he knows from practical experience what it is he is actually judging.

The star in his firmament is, pre-eminently, Yves Saint Laurent. He believes, as does the author of this book, that Saint Laurent is the most important and influential couturier of the second half of the twentieth century, not only for his fashion, but also for his social impact. As Gaultier says, 'Saint Laurent was not as spectacular as Cardin but he was much stronger because he understood structure and shape. He is directly in line of descent from Chanel.'

Gaultier admires Chanel and also claims, 'I loved Jean Muir. The clothes she did were always so strong and clear. In the seventies, Rykiel was like Saint Laurent for me, she did revolutionary things, but quietly. When they are good, women in fashion are better than men because they really have something to say. Even to fight for. And they can say it just right whereas men in fashion are more decorative or too abstract in the way they design. The people I admire most are not extravagant. Too many designers are like that – superficial and missing the point. Clothes must have something to say if they are to be strong. They are not art. They are a reflection of everything that is happening, all around, in society. Success is about choosing just the right moment, so that people say, "yes, that is *it*", even if they didn't realize it before. Dior did it with the New Look and so did Saint Laurent with his mannish dress and his nudity (which I adore). He was just right for the sexual revolution. Bravo.'

'Nowadays', he continues, 'people don't really relate to the clothes in a fashion show. They view the show like a video or a movie because they see it on television. They don't talk about a particular dress and say, "I should love to wear that"; instead they comment on other things – "the music was good"; the models – "I liked that one but not the other"; they

SCARIFICATION has been used by the people in Africa and the South Seas for centuries. In the mid-nineties, its beauty began to interest fashion designers and Jean Paul Gaultier was in the forefront of those adapting it to Western dress, as part of the increasing use of decorative patterning to simulate tattoos (*above*) Spring-Summer 1997 and (*right*) Spring-Summer 1998. (*Photos: Niall McInerney*)

LES FRERES JACQUES, (*above*) a forties popular music-hall act, always wore top hats. It is a theme frequently taken up by Gaultier but, as these pictures show, although he is known for his outrageous experiments on the catwalk, the designer's considerable world sales are a reflection of his ability to make beautifully wearable clothes for men as well as women. These garments are always impeccably cut, such as the two outfits on the far right. (*Photos: Niall McInerney*)

aren't terribly interested in the clothes. The show doesn't do the job it was originally invented for – to relate the clothes to the people. We're in a very strange moment, with both fashion and the media. It's the show that counts – as entertainment, like a TV spectacular. It isn't fashion, any more than the costumes I did for Yvette Horner's show at the Casino de Paris in 1991.' Horner, one of Gaultier's great loves, is a music-hall singer from the old days of French music hall, who accompanies herself on an accordion, as she has always done throughout a long career. She is now well over seventy but is still, for Gaultier, a talisman of the true spirit of France, undiluted by international infiltrations, and as far removed from

SUMMER 1992 was a cosmopolitan collection dedicated to the simple, clean and modern lines of men's tailoring at its best (*above*). Two examples from the Winter 1996–7 collection (*right and centre*); and a sharp suited look from the 1991–2 collection (named after the TV series *The Prisoner*), shown in Florence – a first for Gaultier (*far right*). (*Photos: Niall McInerney*)

transatlantic influences as it is possible for a popular entertainer to be. Her importance to Gaultier is as a reminder of his true cultural beliefs.

Jean Paul Gaultier enjoys visiting New York for many of the reasons which pull him back to London so frequently. It has become part of his annual rhythm to try to go there at least once a year. He loves its energy but knows he could never he happy living there because he feels its driving force is not creativity, but money-making. As Lionel Vermeil has said, 'Money is really not so important to Jean Paul Gaultier. He could stop now and live on very little. There are virtually no luxuries in his life. They don't interest him. All he needs in a flat is a bed, TV and a kitchen.

NAOMI CAMPBELL demonstrates a fold out jewelled triptych in brilliant colours, used to stunning effect on a simple black background and shown in Gaultier's collection for Winter 1997–98, a collection dedicated to Black culture and Black power, which paid tribute to Nina Simone, Miriam Makeba and featuring 'chic rappers'. (*Photo: Niall McInerney*)

He is a man of the streets who loves walking and looking. What he sees on the street always stimulates his imagination. We are talking of a man of very simple tastes and no pretensions. He doesn't even have his own table or desk in the workrooms. He just finds a corner wherever he can. He loves the ambience of the workrooms, the intensity of concentration and quiet discovery. He loves to be part of that. But he is simply not like other couturiers. He doesn't feel the need to fill his space with perfect white flowers and hang beautiful pictures of his clothes or his portrait by famous photographers. He's a very plain, ordinary man, in everything but designing clothes.'

All dress designers have a catalyst for a new collection but, although they know that he's right, few are as honest as Jean Paul Gaultier who admits that his starting point is 'fear – a *slight* fear – that I won't have any ideas. So, I start amassing folders into which I put anything which interests me – for example, a photograph – but not usually of fashion – or a Xerox from a book or magazine. That calms me down because I have something to fall back on, even if I don't use it in the end. It could even be a fabric or colour. Or perhaps a tiny piece of embroidery. With them I'm not too frightened to start. The next stage is never the same. I might find that a theme comes instantly; sometimes I find it later, after I have made decisions about fabrics – and sometimes I think No theme. It's closing my imagination. *Bon*. It will be what it will be, or it won't be. But it will be clothes. Which is what it *must* be!'

Once he starts to draw, he mentally pigeon-holes what he is doing – 'that will be good' – 'that may be OK' – all the time directing his thoughts towards a final effect, which changes and grows as he selects the most likely drawings. 'When I'm dividing my ideas,' he says. 'Then I become much more specific. I am working on parallel lines by then: I have a theme, perhaps, but I also have the fabric – and ideas often come from that. But it doesn't have to be anything very concrete. Sometimes, it remains as just a feeling in my head. I make clothes, not themes.'

'I always react to fabric. It's vital to understand how it behaves. Sometimes, it works well in a small amount but loses its quality if it's used too big. It might be stiffer than I want. Or too soft. All the time everything is changing and I am adapting. Often I end up at a completely different

A PERKY SCARLET denim two-piece and a pert hat are used by Gaultier for a sexy, young combination in his Summer 1992 collection.
(Photo: Niall McInerney)

MASTERY OF MATERIALS and perfection of cut are the basic skills demanded of fashion, whether in tailoring or dressmaking. Gaultier has them both. An extravagently waisted cut-away tail coat from his 'French Can-Can' collection Autumn-Winter 1991–2 (*right*). For Spring-Summer 1992, Gaultier presented a collection dedicated to elegance which featured his own special mixture of traditional and modernism, as in this figure-hugging, corset-string tango dress (*far right*). (*Photos: Niall McInerney*)

'It is not easy when you are surrounded by beautiful people to feel secure'

point from where I started. Then, I worry that I am being too flexible. If you adapt too much it can be that you're not as positive as you must be to create a collection.'

Jean Paul Gaultier works with a team of about a dozen assistants and an *atelier* staff of the same number – although that goes up to around forty when the serious work for the collection begins. His ready-to-wear – for men and women – is made in Italy by Alberta Ferretti but the couture is all done in Paris.

'I am very well organized for ready-to-wear,' he claims. 'Because I work well ahead. Even before the show in Paris I will have been to Milan to begin looking at fabrics for the next season. It's necessary. It takes time, this process. It can be up to three weeks before the samples begin to come through. So, it's probably a month before we can have the first fitting. Even then, it is mainly to see if the fabric is right.

The elements of chic can be very simple in the hands of a skilled designer. Here, Gaultier uses nothing more sophisticated than a blazer, striped and spotted fabrics and a wrap-around belt to produce a fresh and lively young look for Spring-Summer 1992. There is no designer who can take dress clichés and rework them as successfully as Jean Paul Gaultier, who can give even traditional elements a fresh new look by his clever juxtapositions.
(*Photo: Niall McInerney*)

It's only then that I can begin to finalize the shape because, if the fabric doesn't behave as I expect, then I won't get the shape I want. It may seem surprising, but it takes the six months between collections to do everything. Even then the time flies.'

Jean Paul Gaultier is the absolute leader of his company. All decisions are his. He even personally checks the seating for the show. But he often has to fight to get his way, especially with the heads of his *ateliers*. Madame Jacqueline, who is responsible for *flou* – the romantic evening dresses – is a stickler from the old school and the epitome of old-style Parisienne chic with her black hair and black dress. She started with Dior in the forties, worked with Yves Saint Laurent and Chanel and has a very strong personality. She has frequently been appalled at what Jean Paul has wanted to show as couture. To her agonized cry 'This is not couture!', he replies, 'What IS?' Then they have a huge, very French, wordy argument. He wins. She grumbles that, in a long career in couture, she's never been asked to do such hard things as Gaultier demands. But she is steeped in the disciplines of couture, it is her passion, and, even though she calls every dress 'her monster', she does them.

WITH ALL THE GRAVITY and richness of an infanta, the model's rich, high-waisted dress has a timeless magnificence which will still be powerful years from now. It was one of the highlights of the second 'Gaultier Paris' haute couture presentations for Autumn-Winter 1997–8. (*Photo: Niall McInerney*)

Madame Jacqueline's corresponding premiere in tailoring, Madame Anise, came to Gaultier after working for Yves Saint Laurent and Givenchy. She also brings years of experience to her job. Like Jacqueline, she is frequently shocked by Gaultier's demands. She may take a while to be persuaded but, after that, her skill and knowledge mean she is rarely beaten by a technical problem, no matter how unconventional the proposed idea.

As is to be expected of a man like Jean Paul Gaultier, the unconventional almost becomes the commonplace in his house. His approach to the show is a classic example of brinksmanship. Hating routine and loving spontaneity, he keeps things close to his chest for as long as possible. He rarely has a rehearsal and the models appear for the show having no idea of what it is about. They don't know what they will wear. They haven't even seen the catwalk. This approach was learned, according to Vermeil, in Gaultier's early days at Cardin: 'Cardin never decided which girl would wear what. It was simply a matter of time. The first girl ready wore the first outfit on the rail, the second girl got the

Two Gaultier evening looks which show the twin sides of his designing character. A classically understated shape is given an Eastern opulence by rich embroidery whilst a *jeune fille* silhouette in camouflage gives a new dimension to a cliché of femininity by its associations with the predominantly masculine world of warfare. From his Spring-Summer 2000 couture collection. (*Photos: Niall McInerney*)

For his 'Mad Max' collection of Autumn-Winter 1995–6, Gaultier padded and inflated his evening gowns to 'push the Amazon silhouette to the limit of caricature'. (*Photos: Niall McInerney*)

GAULTIER'S MODERNIZATION of the Can-Can look for his Autumn-Winter 1991–2 collection.
(*Photos: Niall McInerney*)

IF PROOF WERE NEEDED that Jean Paul Gaultier approaches fashion in ways uniquely his own, then these pages provide it. Who but Gaultier would create an evening dress from leather? From his Spring-Summer 1998 couture collection.

second one, and so on. Out on the runway. Back. OK. Next one. Same routine. Jean Paul loves to have adventures so he tells the girls virtually nothing more specific than, "If there's a space, fill it." He might set the mood by saying, "You're in a club", but nothing more elaborate. He hates them being "too cinema". He prefers them to look as if they're walking down the street.'

And, of course, he has no preconceived ideas of beauty or what a model's figure should be like. He enjoys mixing people on the runway. His friend Anna still models for him and so does Evelyne Tremois, in her late seventies, who is frequently paired on the catwalk with twenty-eight year old Scott Benoit, in a classic example of what Gaultier described in the eighties as an oscillation between different worlds – a concept not limited to age alone in Gaultier's approach but also including male and female or First and Third Worlds.

Gaultier brings the same pluralist thinking to his choice of area for his headquarters, which are now based in an old furniture factory in Faubourg St Antoine, just off the Place de la Bastille, symbol of the triumph of common sense over ritual. It was once a street of artisans, mainly working in the furniture trade and is now a strangely mixed area. Shops sell cheap furniture which tries to look grand. Cut-price carpet stores rub shoulders with bars where traditional old ladies drink and argue while old men looking like William Burroughs sit, philosophical, world-weary and resigned. Nothing surprises, nothing disappoints. It is an area into which Jean Paul Gaultier slips with perfect ease.

Gaultier once told a journalist, 'When I am truly, truly certain, I am obstinate.' A man of original and fearless approach, Jean Paul is a man who hides his seriousness behind a facetious facade – a facade which frequently drops during conversation to reveal a piercing intelligence. An originator, many of the current freedoms now enjoyed by young designers were first articulated by him in his twenty-year fight against the sterile and commonplace. Totally modern, his questionings, subversions and realizations lead us forward, without ever looking back. Jean Paul Gaultier has remained a question mark in the aesthetics of Paris fashion for twenty years. In another twenty years, it will become apparent how powerful a presence he has been.

EVEN TRADITIONAL APPROACHES to the male suit can be subverted by colour, surface pattern and an exotic choice of fabric, but when suits like these go into production much of the exuberence is stripped from them and what is left is a cut and proportion with universal appeal. *(Photos: Niall McInerney)*

ALL THREE IMAGES are from Gaultier's menswear collection for Spring-Summer 1998, dedicated to the machismo elegance of the flamenco dancer. It marked a new approach to men's tailoring, based on a slim, fitted silhouette. (*Photos: Niall McInerney*)

At the end of the day, designers like Jean Paul Gaultier, famed for fireworks, fun and unexpected frissons on the runway, only become successful by creating beautiful clothes which make women in their thousands sigh with delight – as these three perfect models do. Clothes like these remind us that being a fashion designer is about pleasing the senses – something Gaultier has consistently done since he first began. His Spring-Summer 1998 women's collection was an homage to Frida Kahlo, artist and wife of Diego Rivera, and exemplified the elegance of South America, showing the influence of dress styles from Mexico, Brazil, Argentina and Cuba.
(*Photos: Niall McInerney*)

'I am not an artist. I am an artisan'